CC

MW01030445

WHY INVEST?   **3**
The Battle against Inflation   4
The Power of Compounding   5

**PHYSICAL AND
FINANCIAL ASSETS**   **7**
Liquidity   8
Other Risks   10
The Importance of
Diversification   12

GETTING STARTED   **15**
Developing Your
Investment Plan   16
Asset Allocations for
Different Stages of Life   16
The Importance of
a Mix of Assets   18
Easing the Tax Burden   20

STOCKS   **23**
Characteristics   24
Fundamental vs.
Technical Analysis   24
Assessing a Stock   25
Some Key Ratios   25
Ways to Group Stocks   26
Individual Stock Selection   28
Looking at Small and
Midsized Companies   30
Market Indexes   31
The Appeal of Index Funds   31

Dollar Cost Averaging   35
Dividend Reinvestment Plans   36
Preferred Stock   36
Some Do's and Don't's   36

FIXED-INCOME INVESTMENTS   **39**
Characteristics   40
Credit Ratings   41
Other Factors Affecting Price   42
Reinvestment Rate Risk   43
Some Types of Bonds   44

MUTUAL FUNDS   **47**
Characteristics   48
Open-End versus
Closed-End Funds   49
Fees   49
International Choices   50

**BROKERS AND THE
SECURITIES MARKETS**   **53**
Functions of Exchanges   54
The Nasdaq Stock Market   54
Regulations for the
Securities Industry   54
Role of the Broker   55
Types of Orders   55

Glossary   **57**
Standard & Poor's Products   **61**
Additional Reading   **64**

TABLES AND CHARTS

Table 1   4
Total Returns of Various
Asset Classes

Table 2   6
The Power of Compounding

Table 3   9
How Total Returns from
Different Types of Investments
Compare

Table 4   18
Sample Investment Allocations
for Different Investor Age
Groups

Table 5   21
Tax-Exempt versus Taxable
Yields

Table 6   29
Performance of Selected S&P
Industry Stock Groups

Table 7   31
Characteristics of S&P 500
and S&P MidCap 400 Indexes

Table 8   35
An Example of Dollar Cost
Averaging

Table 9   48
Long-Term Characteristics
of Mutual Funds

Table 10   51
Annual Performance of Various
National Stock Markets

Chart 1   10
The Risk-Reward Tradeoff

Chart 2   11
Annual Total Returns of
Stocks and Bonds

Chart 3   12
The Best/Worst Total Returns
(1926-96)

Chart 4   32
Long-Term Performance
of S&P 500

Chart 5   43
Annual Inflation-Adjusted Total
Returns of U.S. Government
Securities

WHY INVEST?

People choose to spend their money in many ways. The bulk of most people's income goes for day-to-day living expenses—food, shelter, and clothing. But even if you live a no-frills lifestyle, it is important to make some investments for the future. A relatively small sum set aside each year can make an important contribution to your long-term financial security.

Investing often involves deferring or giving up current consumption. This is done to increase wealth and build future purchasing power. For example, to buy 100 shares of a stock, a vacation might be postponed. If the investment is successful, however, the profits from it could fund future vacations or a year of a child's college education.

Specific investment decisions should be based on a consideration of risk versus reward. Some investments are riskier than others, and investors' tolerance for risk varies. In general, greater risk to the investor should be offset by probability or potential for a greater reward—a greater return on investment. The return is simply the profit earned on the investment, including capital gains and any interest or dividend payments. Returns are typically reported in pretax dollars.

This publication is a guide to investing, with an emphasis on understanding stocks, bonds, and mutual funds. A qualified investment professional can help you establish a portfolio tailored to your situation, but the more knowledgeable you are about investing, the more likely you are to be successful at it.

The Battle against Inflation

Investments can provide a way to keep up with or stay ahead of inflation. While inflation rates have fallen sharply from the peak levels of 1979-80, the dollar is still shrinking in value. A dollar squirreled away in a safe-deposit box in 1980 had only about 52 cents of buying power in early 1997. Although every investment

TABLE 1: TOTAL RETURNS OF VARIOUS ASSET CLASSES, 1926-96
            (Compound annual rates)

	In current dollars	In inflation-adjusted (real) $	Standard deviation
Common stocks	10.7%	7.4%	20.3
Corporate bonds	5.6%	2.4%	8.7
U.S. Treasury bills	3.7%	0.6%	3.3

All returns are in pretax dollars. Common stocks represent the performance of the S&P 500 Composite Stock Price Index, with dividends reinvested. Corporate bonds are long-term, with interest reinvested. U.S. Treasury bills are three-month U.S. government debt, with interest reinvested. Inflation represents the Consumer Price Index. Standard deviation measures the risk, or volatility, of rates of return in current dollars.

Source: Ibbotson Associates.

carries some risk, it may be even more hazardous not to invest.

An investment's so-called real rate of return is measured in terms of purchasing power, which is the nominal rate of profit growth adjusted downward for inflation. Among the kinds of investments shown in Table 1, common stocks historically have provided the best gains in purchasing power over the long term, followed by corporate bonds. U.S. Treasury bills, considered the safest investment of the three listed, recorded a compound annual rate of return of 3.7% over the period from 1926 to 1996, barely outpacing inflation.

The Power of Compounding

Getting started with investing as early as possible can make a big difference in how much wealth is ultimately accumulated. The benefits of saving early in life are greatly magnified by compounding. In this process, the growth of an investment's value is computed on the sum of the original investment, including the assumption that dividends or interest are reinvested in the same asset. For example, consider two individuals who can both receive a 10% compound annual return on their investment over a 40-year period. Let's suppose the first person puts in $2,000 a year for the first eight years, representing a total investment of $16,000, and then stops. At the end of 40 years, earnings from the original investment will have ballooned to $515,188 because of compounding. Meanwhile, let's suppose the second individual invests nothing for the first 8 years, then $2,000 annually for 32 years (Years 9 through 40), representing a total investment of $64,000. At the end of 40 years, despite having put in four times as much capital, the second individual's earnings will amount to $378,496—less than 75% of that of the first individual, who started earlier (see Table 2).

The amount of wealth accumulated is also substantially affected by seemingly small differences in the annual rate of return. For example, a $10,000 initial investment, with nothing added to it other than the reinvestment of earnings, will grow to $46,610 over 20 years if the compound annual rate of return is 8%. If the rate of return is 10%, however, that same initial investment of $10,000 will increase to $67,275—or 44% more.

TABLE 2: THE POWER OF COMPOUNDING

If you invest $2,000 a year for the first eight years of a 40-year period with annual compounding at 10%, you will earn more than someone who invests $2,000 a year from years nine through 40. The latter's total contribution would be four times greater, yet it would earn 27% less.

Year	EARLY FUNDING Contribution	EARLY FUNDING Year-end Value	LATE FUNDING Contribution	LATE FUNDING Year-end Value
1	$2,000	$2,200	$0	$0
2	2,000	4,620	0	0
3	2,000	7,282	0	0
4	2,000	10,210	0	0
5	2,000	13,431	0	0
6	2,000	16,974	0	0
7	2,000	20,871	0	0
8	2,000	25,158	0	0
9	0	27,674	2,000	2,200
10	0	30,441	2,000	4,620
11	0	33,485	2,000	7,282
12	0	36,834	2,000	10,210
13	0	40,517	2,000	13,431
14	0	44,569	2,000	16,974
15	0	49,026	2,000	20,871
16	0	53,929	2,000	25,158
17	0	59,322	2,000	29,874
18	0	65,254	2,000	35,061
19	0	71,779	2,000	40,767
20	0	78,957	2,000	47,044
21	0	86,853	2,000	53,948
22	0	95,583	2,000	61,643
23	0	105,092	2,000	69,897
24	0	115,601	2,000	79,087
25	0	127,161	2,000	89,196
26	0	139,877	2,000	100,316
27	0	153,865	2,000	112,548
28	0	169,252	2,000	126,003
29	0	186,177	2,000	140,803
30	0	204,795	2,000	157,083
31	0	225,275	2,000	174,991
32	0	247,803	2,000	194,690
33	0	272,583	2,000	216,359
34	0	299,841	2,000	240,195
35	0	329,825	2,000	266,415
36	0	362,808	2,000	295,257
37	0	399,089	2,000	326,983
38	0	438,998	2,000	361,881
39	0	482,898	2,000	400,269
40	0	531,188	2,000	442,496
Investment		**$16,000**		**$64,000**
Earnings		**$515,188**		**$378,496**

Source: S&P's The Outlook.

PHYSICAL AND FINANCIAL ASSETS

There are many kinds of assets in which people can invest. Physical assets—those that are tangible—constitute one category. This includes items such as houses, coins, and works of art. Some physical assets, such as a house, can both meet current living needs and serve as an investment, since house prices have historically risen in value over time. Also, physical assets often provide their owners with an emotional return that is separate from any financial reward. Examples include the pride of home ownership and the sense of beauty that a work of art can bring.

Financial assets, a second category, include stocks and bonds issued by companies to raise capital for the operation and expansion of their businesses. After the initial sale is completed, these securities are often available for resale through markets such as the New York Stock Exchange (NYSE). In addition to stocks and bonds, various other financial assets are readily available to the public. Among them are debt securities issued by the federal, state, and local governments; money market funds; traditional bank accounts; certificates of deposit; mutual funds; options; and futures.

While financial assets represent much more than just pieces of paper, they are an indirect and less tangible form of wealth. Another way in which financial assets differ from physical assets is that they often generate cash income for the owners in the form of dividend or interest payments. Physical assets, in contrast, may require cash outlays during the period in which they are owned. For example, maintenance, repairs, and insurance on a building must be paid by the owner. However, a primary investment aim of owning either physical or financial assets is to be able to sell them at some future time for more than it cost to acquire them.

As indicated in Table 3, the returns of different assets vary from year to year. However, in the long-term, stocks have historically outperformed most other asset classes.

Liquidity

Some spectacular gains in value have come from physical assets. During portions of the past two decades, real estate prices boomed and rare-art auctions generated record prices. As prices paid for these physical assets began to soften toward the end of the 1980s, however, a significant drawback became more apparent: a lack of liquidity. Whereas most financial assets can be bought or sold at a moment's notice, it's harder to sell a physical asset such as a house. This is largely because huge quantities of financial assets are bought and sold every day and the marketplace for them is a national one. Furthermore, for any given company, one share of common stock is identical to every other. Often, in a single day, such shares have hundreds of buyers and sellers who establish, through their transactions, the current value of the asset. In contrast, a house or a painting is generally a unique asset; nothing else exactly like it is available for sale. This quality of uniqueness adds to the complexity of finding a buyer and seller who can agree on a sale price for the asset.

How readily an asset can be turned into cash—the ease with which buyers and sellers can be brought together and can agree on a price—is called liquidity. Assets that are less liquid tend to have a wider spread between the "bid" (the price offered by a would-be buyer) and the "ask" (the seller's asking price). Among financial assets, some are more liquid than others—an important consideration in assessing risk. Some limited partnerships, for example, have little or no liquidity and should be bought only with the expectation of holding them until maturity. The illiquidity of such partnership interests largely reflects the absence of a public market for the trading of partnership shares. In addition, the structure and assets (e.g. specific pieces of real estate) of such partnerships may be tailored to the financial needs of a relatively small group of investors, which may narrow the resale potential of a partnership interest. In contrast, money market funds, a type of mutual fund that invests in short-term debt instruments, are so liquid they are considered to be cash equivalents. Most brokerage firms will automatically place your uninvested funds in a money market fund, where you will earn a slightly better rate of return than you would

TABLE 3: HOW TOTAL RETURNS FROM DIFFERENT TYPES OF ASSETS COMPARE (Percent Change)

Asset category	1993	1994	1995	1996
Stocks				
Dow Jones Industrial Average	18.05	5.88	36.87	29.11
S&P 500 Index	9.99	1.29	37.57	22.98
Bonds				
Long-Term Treasuries[1]	16.93	-7.64	30.71	-0.81
Intermediate-Term Treasuries[2]	7.81	-1.76	14.48	3.99
Money Market Funds	2.70	2.44	2.86	2.70
Gold	17.80	-2.00	1.00	-5.10
Residential Real Estate[3]	NA	2.40	4.20	3.20
Art[4]	2.60	-17.20	9.40	-1.30
Rare Coins[5]	-0.26	-2.91	0.38	4.09

[1]Lehman Brothers Long-Term Treasury Index. [2]Lehman Brothers Intermediate-Term Treasury Index.
[3]Office of Federal Housing Enterprise (Repeat Sale Index; third quarter vs. third quarter). [4]Daily Telegraph Art 100 Index. [5]Top Investment grade (Coin World Trends Survey).

Source: The Wall Street Journal.

with a savings account at a bank, and your money will normally be immediately available.

Other Risks

All prospective investments should be evaluated in terms of the trade-offs between risk and reward (see Chart 1). The expected return on an investment may be based largely on its historical performance, but, because there is no guarantee that the future will repeat the past, you should assess the possibility that you won't reap your target profit.

One measure of risk and return is the range of possible outcomes. With a U.S. Treasury bond, you are assured of getting a series of modest interest payments and your principal (the amount of your initial invest-

ment) will be preserved if you hold the bond to maturity. With the riskiest of investments, such as the speculative purchase of a stock option, you may quadruple your money—or you may lose it all. In addition to the matter of liquidity, there are at least three other kinds of risk to consider—credit risk, interest rate risk, and price volatility.

Credit risk and interest rate risk are the primary concerns with bonds and other fixed-income securities. The role that each of these two risks plays varies according to the type of investment. U.S. government securities, for example, have very little credit risk because it is highly unlikely that the federal government will default on its commitment to pay interest and principal on debt. Because of this low credit risk, the long-term rate of return on such government securities

CHART 1: THE RISK-REWARD TRADEOFF

The return from various investment choices tends to vary according to the risk.

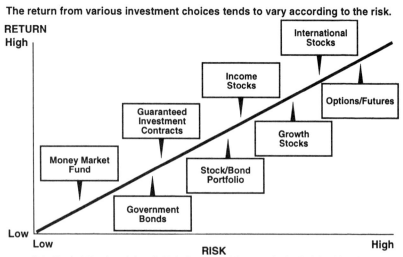

Note: The depiction above is intended to indicate general, long-term levels of relative risk and return.

tends to be lower than that available with other investments. Government securities, however, do share a risk with other fixed-income instruments—the interest rate risk. If an investor elects to sell such a security prior to maturity, the market price will depend largely on the prevailing interest rate environment. If rates have risen since the security was purchased, the investor will likely have to sell the security for less than the purchase price.

Another measure of risk is price volatility. Although prices for bonds and other fixed-income investments fluctuate as interest rates change, these fluctuations are usually small. Even though normally less volatile than the options market, stock market returns do vary widely. As a result, investors in the stock market should have a longer time frame and a greater risk tolerance than is advised for some other, less volatile forms of investment. Although historical returns on long-term stock investments have been relatively high, stock prices tend to move more rapidly and to greater extremes than prices of most other kinds of financial assets. Potential stock market investors should reflect on how much their financial and emotional comfort could be tested in periods of declining prices. Charts 2 and 3 below show the annual total returns of stocks and corporate bonds, plus the volatility within each year, for a recent 20-year period. During the 1980s, in particular, the return from bonds was unusually high, largely due to declines in interest rates.

In an extreme example, the stock market declined more than 20% in value on a single day in October

CHART 2: ANNUAL TOTAL RETURNS OF STOCKS AND BONDS

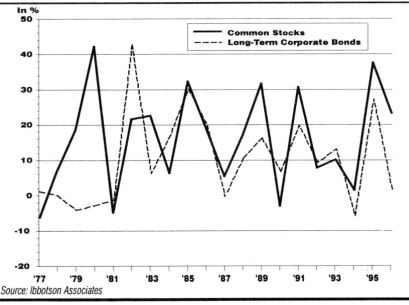

Source: Ibbotson Associates

11

1987, wiping out the gains of more than two years. Investors shaken by this experience may have sold their shares and put their money into a safe haven, such as a money market fund. In doing so, however, they would have missed out on the above average gains from stocks that followed. If $10,000 had been left in the stock market following that dramatic 1987 decline, it would have grown to about $23,000 in value by the end of 1993, assuming the reinvestment of dividends. In comparison, the same $10,000 in a money market fund would have grown to only roughly $14,000. Of course, there have been other periods, of even five years and longer, when stocks have declined in value and the returns from other safer, or less volatile, kinds of investments would have been significantly better. But for investors who have a

long-term time horizon and who are willing to ride out the volatility, history indicates that to earn a high return, a meaningful portion of their invested capital should be in stocks.

The Importance of Diversification

Diversification of investment holdings is the most important shield against risk. Because some investments rise in value while others fall, diversification smooths out much of the volatility of the overall return from a portfolio. Diversification sacrifices some of the upside potential, but this should be more than offset by the benefits of a lower level of risk.

The point is: Don't put all of your eggs in one basket. Although the

CHART 3: THE BEST/WORST TOTAL RETURNS (1926-96)

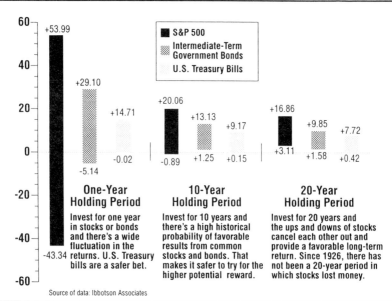

	One-Year Holding Period	10-Year Holding Period	20-Year Holding Period
	Invest for one year in stocks or bonds and there's a wide fluctuation in the returns. U.S. Treasury bills are a safer bet.	Invest for 10 years and there's a high historical probability of favorable results from common stocks and bonds. That makes it safer to try for the higher potential reward.	Invest for 20 years and the ups and downs of stocks cancel each other out and provide a favorable long-term return. Since 1926, there has not been a 20-year period in which stocks lost money.

Source of data: Ibbotson Associates

attractiveness of stocks over the long term is stressed in this publication, all your investment capital should not go into this class of assets. In addition, you should diversify your holdings even within each class of assets. For instance, a list of 20 stocks, spread across different industries, provides adequate diversification for an equity portfolio. To diversify a fixed-income portfolio, securities should be held with different risk levels and different dates of maturity.

Anyone with less than $20,000 to invest in stocks or bonds should seriously consider mutual funds because of the diversification they provide. Also, for both small and large investors, placing some money in funds can offer relief from the task of selecting individual securities. (For a fuller discussion of mutual funds, see Page 48.)

GETTING STARTED

Developing Your Investment Plan

Money should be set aside for certain things before it is spent on security investments. For example, adequate life, disability, and medical insurance should be purchased. Home ownership should also be a priority in many cases, particularly since interest payments on a home mortgage loan are often an important tax deduction. You should also maintain some cash reserves for emergencies.

After these requirements have been met, you can begin to develop your investment plan. Think carefully about the kinds of assets that are appropriate to your objectives and risk tolerance. In addition, you need to consider your time horizon: When will you need or want to spend your money? Identify your objectives; preservation of principal, current income, or long-term capital gains may be among them. Then assess your ability to bear risk by making a careful assessment of your personal financial position, taking into account age, family responsibilities, income level, cash flow, and tax considerations. Even your temperament has a bearing on your risk tolerance. If you are a worrier, confine your commitments to relatively safe securities. Peace of mind means a great deal.

Once you have weighed all of these factors and considerations, you are ready to set up some parameters for your portfolio. A qualified financial advisor can help you determine an appropriate way to allocate your assets. If you do not already have a stock broker, ask someone whose professional judgment you trust to recommend one. Investors with large sums to invest may wish to find an advisor with estate-planning expertise.

Asset Allocations for Different Stages of Life

Some generalizations can be made about what kind of financial assets are appropriate for people at different stages of their lives. Usually, young adults with a lengthy time horizon and a growing income potential should be willing and able to assume more risk than older people who are nearing or are in retirement. Even for people in their 70s and 80s, however, a small commitment to aggressive investments, such as stocks, may make sense. People are living longer, and the prospect of above-average returns may be too important to forgo completely.

Also, there may be occasions when the time horizon for the money being invested does not match up with the age of the investor. For example, an elderly grandparent may be planning to make an annual gift to a young grandchild, with the intention that the assets be used to help pay for a college education 15 years in the future, when the grandparent may no longer be alive. In such a case, the lengthy time horizon for these funds might be a good argument that they be invested in stocks. However, if the money was targeted, instead, for the grandparent's shorter-term living expenses, a safer, but potentially less rewarding investment—such as a money market account—would probably be more appropriate.

The time horizon for the individual and the specific investment should be important considerations in determining asset allocations and how much short-term price fluctuation, or risk, a person is willing to take. However, the objective for an investment may also have a bearing on risk tolerance. For example, an investor may be more cautious with money which is intended for medical care than he or she would be with funds which are targeted for an extravagant vacation.

For many young adults a major financial goal is the purchase of a home. The need to accumulate enough capital to make a down payment temporarily shortens the time horizon for this group of investors. Such investors may want to emphasize conservative shorter-term fixed-income securities instead of ones that aim for long-term capital gains. Also, they may need to abandon temporarily the goal of maximizing their after-tax return on investment. For them, placing large sums in tax-deferred retirement accounts with penalties for early withdrawal may be impractical.

Once the house has been purchased, however, an appropriate portfolio for young to middle-aged investors might be weighted heavily toward growth-oriented stocks or mutual funds, as well as conservative blue-chip stocks, with the long-term goal of capital gains. Such an asset allocation could help to build wealth for other big-ticket items, such as vacations, children's college educa-

tions, and the even longer-term prospect of retirement.

People in the peak earning years of 35 to 60 are likely to have more capital available for investment. With income relatively high, it is advisable to place a growing emphasis on deferring taxes or sheltering at least a portion of the earnings. (See Easing the Tax Burden, Page 20.) Alternatives such as 401(k) accounts and Individual Retirement Accounts (IRAs) are likely to be increasingly attractive. If your tax bracket is high enough, municipal bonds should have a relatively heavy weighting in your taxable investment accounts. Such tax-exempt securities are inappropriate for 401(k) and IRA accounts, however, which already offer tax-saving features.

Most investors should move gradually toward more cash and more conservative kinds of intermediate- and short-term bonds as they get closer to retirement. In their later years, people often become less risk tolerant. Income levels often decline following retirement, and the investor has less time to recover principal if an investment does not work out as expected. If you depend on income from investments for a large part of your living expenses, your main objective should be assured income and the relative safety of principal. The securities best suited for this purpose are U.S. government issues and high-grade corporate bonds. The fixed nature of the income received from such investments, however, limits the amount of protection they provide against inflation. To achieve some protection of purchasing power, it is advisable to make a relatively small,

TABLE 4: SAMPLE INVESTMENT ALLOCATION FOR DIFFERENT INVESTOR AGE GROUPS

Kind of Investment	Age 20–35	Age 35–50	Age 50–65	Age 65+
Aggressive growth stocks (Int'l. & small companies)	40%	30%	20%	10%
Total-return stocks (Large blue-chip U.S. companies)	40%	40%	30%	25%
Bonds	10%	20%	30%	40%
Cash equivalents (Money market, CDs)	10%	10%	20%	25%
TOTAL	100%	100%	100%	100%

*An individual's tax bracket should be a major consideration in determining the level of investment in municipal bonds. The table above assumes that income levels rise until age 65.

but not insignificant, allotment to common stocks. Selections should be confined to high-quality issues, preferably with attractive dividend yields.

Table 4 shows a sample allocation among investment choices for investors aged 20-35, 35-50, 50-65, and more than 65. The distribution of investments illustrates some generalities about portfolio management and how investors' asset allocations tend to change over time. Since the information presented is only intended as an example, the ideal asset allocation for any individual can vary greatly from the samples given.

The sample allocations do not show contributions to tax-advantaged retirement plans. Ideally, assets in such accounts are also growing until retirement, when these investments are included as part of an overall investment plan. Other systematic savings programs, such as Employee Stock Ownership Plans (ESOPs) with automatic paycheck deductions, can also provide a good way to accumulate capital.

The Importance of a Mix of Assets

The way in which funds are allocated among various asset categories is the most important long-run determinant of the return on investment. Different assets perform well during different economic periods. For example, in the late 1970s and early 1980s, gold was a hot investment. Prices peaked at about $850 an ounce in 1980, up from only $100 less than four years earlier. During this period, when inflation was eroding the purchasing power of financial assets, gold was seen as an attractive physical asset to own. Since then, however, gold has generally been one of the weaker investment alternatives. In 1996, the average price of gold was aproximately $388 an ounce, down sharply from 1980's level, and up only about 1% from the average price in 1990. Because an investor cannot perfectly anticipate when to move funds from one asset class to another, it is important to have a diversified approach to investing, one in which funds are continuously committed to a variety of assets.

Changes in economic conditions and investors' perception of them affect investment performance. For example, stock valuations are often a leading indicator of the overall economy. In fact, the S&P 500 Composite Stock Price Index (popularly known as the S&P 500) is a component of the U.S. government's Index of Leading Indicators. Since the economy tends to move in cycles, the stock market does also. When investors expect that the economy is going to strengthen, stock prices often rise in anticipation of better corporate earnings. When the economy is at relatively high levels of activity, however, investors may start anticipating the next recession. As a result, stock prices may decline before the economy actually weakens.

A key factor with bond prices is the direction in which interest rates move. When interest rates rise, bond prices generally decline, and the inverse is also true. Let's look at an example. Assume that a $1,000 bond, priced at par (the face value, which in this case is $1,000), yields 10% (the annual coupon, or interest, payment is $100). Three months later interest rates decline to the extent that similar securities are being issued with a 9.1% yield (the coupon payment is $91 for each $1,000 of principal). In response to the decline in interest rates, the price of the bond with the $100 coupon level is adjusted upward, so that it, too, will provide approximately a 9.1% yield for anyone buying it now. To yield 9.1%, the price has to rise from $1,000 to $1,100. Conversely, if interest rates rise, bond prices decline. For the $100 in annual interest to generate a yield of 11%, for example, the bond would have to drop to a market price of $909.

Some investors seek to time their investments to correspond to market fluctuations, raising or lowering allocations to various asset classes at strategic moments. One means of adjusting asset allocations is to rebalance based on preplanned levels, such as 60% for stocks, 30% for bonds, and 10% for cash. With such an approach, an investor would sell portions of an asset class that appreciated in value, shifting the proceeds to areas that have not fared as well. To some extent, this approach can force you to sell high and buy low. For example, if stock prices rise, the value of your stock holdings might jump from the preplanned 60% of your portfolio to 70%. To get your stock allocation back to the targeted 60%, you would have to sell some of your shares. This could be fortuitous; perhaps the stock market has reached an interim peak. Meanwhile the market value of your bond portfolio may have shrunk to 20% of your financial assets. Proceeds from the sale of stock could be used to increase the bond allocation back to 30%.

In later sections we offer advice on selecting stocks, bonds, and mutual funds. As you choose among the various financial assets, always determine whether you are investing or speculating. Although the line between the two blurs sometimes, an investment is a thought-out commitment of funds from which you expect to receive a reasonable return. Investments typically involve a longer time horizon than speculations; you are willing to let wealth build gradually, rather than looking for a quick bonanza. That doesn't mean you should never speculate; just keep it at an appropriate level, which for most investors means involving no more than 10% of their portfolio.

Easing the Tax Burden

An important consideration for most investors, particularly for those with substantial incomes, is how to soften the impact of income taxes. To encourage investment, capital gains once received preferable income tax treatment. But with the tax law changes in 1986, they are now taxed like regular earned income.

Current tax laws enable people to defer taxes on sizable portions of their income through employer-sponsored 401(k) retirement accounts. Funds contributed from wages (up to an annual limit of $9,500 in 1996) are excluded from current taxable income. In addition, taxes are deferred on income and gains generated while the funds are in the account. Many 401(k) accounts have another attraction: Your employer may contribute to the account, in some cases matching what you are contributing on a dollar-for-dollar basis. The employer's contribution is additional tax-deferred income for you. Similar features are available on other pension accounts, such as 403(b)s, which are commonly used for educators.

For those who qualify, IRAs and Keogh plans also offer tax deferments. Depending on income level and access to employer-sponsored retirement plans, some people are not eligible to receive deductions from their current taxable income for new contributions placed in such accounts. However, everyone who has an IRA or a Keogh plan is entitled to tax deferments on the interest, dividends, and capital gains generated in such accounts until the funds actually are withdrawn, usually following retirement (when taxpayers typically are in a substantially lower tax bracket). Any money withdrawn before age 59-1/2 is usually subject to a 10% early-withdrawal penalty, and you must begin taking withdrawals by age 70-1/2 or you'll also incur penalties.

Much of the money invested in tax-deferred 401(k) plans has been placed in Guaranteed Investment Contracts (GICs), which are a form of investment offered primarily by insurance companies. With a GIC, the issuer offers a rate of return that may be fixed for the entire term of the contract, or that may have a variable component for at least a portion of that time. One appeal of GICs has been the relatively predictable return, at rates above those offered by money market accounts, that investors will receive. The recent financial troubles of several insurers have caused a broad reassessment of the contracts and the insurance companies that offer them. Most major issuing insurance companies, however, continue to have relatively solid financial resources. In general, electing to invest in a GIC should depend largely on the rate of return being offered and the financial strength of the issuing insurance company. A look at the insurance company's credit ratings (see section on Fixed Income Investments) may be helpful in assessing its relative financial strength.

Tax-deferred income can also be generated through policies offered by life insurance companies. The most common example is the single-premium deferred annuity (SPDA), which is largely used as a tool for retirement planning. Investments in SPDAs accrue tax-deferred interest, but withdrawals are subject to the same restrictions as IRAs. As with GICs, you should concern yourself with the quality of the insurance company issuing the SPDA. Other kinds of tax-deferred annuities come in a variety of packages offering a range of investment opportunities. As with other forms of investment, fees and restrictions related to the product should be considered when determining its appeal.

Another type of policy with potential tax benefits offered by life insurance companies is whole life. If an investment in a whole-life policy produces earnings in excess of the premium payment required, the surplus may accrue as tax-deferred savings until the funds are withdrawn. Also, death benefits paid from life insurance policies are tax-exempt for beneficiaries.

Another way to limit income taxes on investments is to purchase municipal bonds issued by state and local governments and their agencies. The interest payments of most municipal bonds are exempt from federal and, in some instances, state and local income taxes. Table 5 shows examples where municipal bond yields are comparable, on an after-tax basis, to

TABLE 5: TAX-EXEMPT VERSUS TAXABLE YIELDS

	\multicolumn{7}{c}{Yields on tax-exempt securities of}						
	3.00%	4.00%	5.00%	6.00%	7.00%	8.00%	9.00%
are equal to the yields below on taxable securities							
15% tax rate	3.53%	4.71%	5.88%	7.06%	8.24%	9.41%	10.59%
28% tax rate	4.17%	5.56%	6.94%	8.33%	9.72%	11.11%	12.50%
31% tax rate	4.35%	5.80%	7.25%	8.70%	10.14%	11.59%	13.04%
36% tax rate	4.69%	6.25%	7.81%	9.38%	10.94%	12.50%	14.06%
39.6% tax rate	4.97%	6.62%	8.28%	9.93%	11.59%	13.25%	14.90%

Note: To compute the equivalent taxable yield for a tax-exempt security, divide the tax-exempt yield by the result of one minus the appropriate tax rate.

other investments whose income is taxable. As with all investments, when comparing various kinds of bonds, it is advisable to look at the prospective after-tax return.

Another way to ease the tax burden is to own stocks that pay relatively low or no dividends. With this approach, an investor can create wealth through long-term capital gains. In such cases, the absence of substantial or any dividend payments will probably be offset by the company's ability to reinvest its earnings profitably in the business. If such a stock rises significantly in price, the investor's tax on the gain is deferred until after the shares are sold.

Furthermore, when securities are inherited by individuals, their taxable basis can change dramatically. For the inheritor, future taxes related to the sale of the securities are based on the market price at the time of inheritance rather than on the price at which the prior owner acquired them. For example, if someone bought a stock 10 years ago at $20 a share and the current market price is $50, that owner would be taxed on a $30 gain if the stock were sold. Assume instead that the stock was not sold but was inherited by someone else at a point in time when the stock's price is $50. If the new owner then sells the stock at that price, there is no tax liability because the new owner has made no gain during the period on the sale of the inherited stock. The new owner's tax basis is the same as the current market price ($50), as opposed to the $20 basis that applied to the previous owner.

However, in general, be sure to look beyond the tax treatment of current payouts. It is always important to choose investments with sound underlying economics.

STOCKS

Characteristics

Stockholders have an ownership interest in a business. Most U.S. businesses are privately owned, but investors can buy shares in more than 10,000 corporations that are publicly traded. This includes most of the titans of industry—such as General Electric and Coca-Cola—as well as many small companies. Today, many millions of people in the U.S. own stock in publicly traded companies or in equity mutual funds that invest in stocks.

When buying stock, an investor is typically hoping that the perceived value of the company will rise, producing a capital gain when the shares are sold later to someone else at a higher price. Capital gains are one of two components that typically constitute the total return from stock investments. Another way in which stock ownership pays a return is through dividends, the portion of a corporation's earnings that is paid to stockholders. To compute a stock's dividend yield, divide the amount of the annual dividend by the current price per share. For example, if a stock is priced at $10 a share and the annual dividend is $0.50 a share, the dividend yield is $0.50/$10.00, or 5%.

There is wide variation in the performance of common stocks—both for the general market and for individual issues. However, as we have already explained, if you can ride out the interim ups and downs (the price volatility), the long-term value of stock market investments tends to grow with the economy. Through 1994, stock prices, as measured by the S&P 500 (an index based on 500 large companies), rose in 16 of the previous 20 years. The annual performance ranged from a 32% rise in 1975 to a 30% decline the year before. Also, holders of common stock received dividends, which averaged more than 4% annually of their investments' market value. Over this 20-year period, the stock market's compound annual total return, including both price increases and dividends, was about 15%. In comparison, consumer prices advanced at about a 5% compound annual rate during the same period.

Fundamental vs. Technical Analysis

One widely used approach to stock market investing is to focus on fundamentals. Fundamentals include factors such as the earnings, cash flow, and balance sheet statistics of a given company, plus general economic conditions and the industry in which the company operates. Such an analysis looks at whether the current valuation of a company, as seen in its stock price, adequately reflects the level of business success perceived for it in the future.

A second approach to investing emphasizes technical factors related to trading activity. A technical analyst, or chartist, attempts to forecast the direction of stock prices by examining their trends. For example, if a stock price breaks above a prior resistance level, it may be headed up further.

Obviously, there is a relationship

between the fundamental and the technical factors. If a stock price has what appears to be upward momentum, this probably reflects favorable fundamental factors, such as a good earnings report from the company or the announcement of a new product. Although an awareness of trading patterns can be helpful in timing investments, technical analysis can be quite specialized, and we suggest that most investors emphasize a fundamental approach to investing.

Assessing a Stock

When looking at a potential stock investment, you might consider several questions: What is the primary business of the company? What is the company's competitive position relative to others in the same industry—does it have clear advantages or disadvantages? What level of market share does it have? How much does its overall business depend on a single customer or on general economic conditions? What are the prospects for growth?

Although the past is not necessarily indicative of future results, it is advisable to examine a company's historical performance. Look at 10-year trends in the company's income statement data, as published, for example, in the Standard & Poor's Stock Reports. Have revenues and profits been generally growing? If not, why? Also, has revenue growth primarily been coming from higher volume, new products, acquisitions, or increased prices? What has the trend in profitability been? Have earnings as a percentage of revenues been on the rise?

Some Key Ratios

Certain ratios can be useful tools in analyzing and comparing companies. Financial ratios provide ways to quantify a company's operating success and financial well-being. Valuation ratios gauge how fairly a stock is priced. The ratios for a given company don't mean much by themselves, but they are very revealing when compared with the company's historical ratios and with the ratios of comparable companies in the same industry. Although the list is far from comprehensive, a look at the following key ratios will help you evaluate a potential investment:

Return on Assets (ROA) and Return on Equity (ROE). Net income (minus preferred stock dividends) divided by average total assets (ROA); and net income divided by average total common equity (ROE). These financial ratios indicate how profitably a company is investing funds from stock offerings, borrowings, and retained earnings. When debt leverage is used effectively (that is, generating a profitable return from borrowed funds), a company's ROE should be higher than its ROA.

Long-Term Debt to Total Capital. Obtained from the balance sheet, this ratio is used to gauge a company's financial strength. (Total capital equals shareholders' equity plus long-term debt; often this analysis is done as a debt to equity ratio.) A "clean" balance sheet has little or no debt. Companies capitalized with 50% debt (a debt to equity ratio of 1:1) or more might be overleveraged; heavy interest payments could limit growth of future earnings and restrict available financing for maintenance or expansion. This concept is similar to looking at the size of a homeowner's mortgage relative to the value of the house. For firms such as utility companies, however, a large proportion of debt, or financial leverage, is typically less of a concern than for other types of companies because utility companies have a relatively predictable and adequate stream of income and cash flow to cover interest expense.

Current Ratio. The relationship between current assets (those that are relatively liquid and/or are likely to be turned into cash within the next year) and current liabilities (payments due within one year). This ratio is especially critical for companies having financial difficulties. For many industrial companies, a ratio in which current assets are at least 1.5 times current liabilities suggests the ability to meet near-term obligations. A ratio of significantly less than that amount could signal a coming cash crunch. However, advisable benchmarks may differ significantly among various industries

Price/Earnings (P/E) Multiple. Price per share divided by earnings per share. This is probably the most widely used valuation ratio. It compares a company's stock price to a recent or future level of earnings per share. When looking at a stock's P/E multiple, investors should compare it with the range of P/Es that same stock has been valued at in the past and with P/Es of other stocks of similar companies. P/E should be evaluated in light of various factors, including the rate of changes in expected future earnings.

Price-to-Book Value. Price per share divided by assets per share. This valuation ratio reveals the value set by the stock market on a company's assets. As with other ratios, the price-to-book ratio can be misleading without further information. For example, if a company's assets are carried on its books at far below their actual current value while another company's assets are overstated, a comparison of the two companies' price-to-book ratios will be distorted.

Ways to Group Stocks

One way that stocks can be grouped is according to trading characteristics. For example, some stocks are perceived as takeover candidates. In general, during speculative periods, these shares are likely to be priced high in relation to earnings. If a takeover does not materialize, however, such stocks are vulnerable to steep declines.

Another kind of stock grouping is blue chips. These stocks represent ownership in high-quality, premier companies, often the leaders in their industries. Such companies have long-established records of earnings and dividend payments and tend to be solid long-term investments.

Stocks can also be categorized by industry. Industries themselves can be grouped by various characteristics that influence stock performance. Although there are exceptions to these stereotypes within any industry, below are some of the major categories often cited by investors:

Cyclical. Industries whose sales and profits are highly sensitive to economic activity are dubbed cyclicals. Many cyclical industries manufacture relatively mature, commodity-like products, such as steel or chemicals. Purchases of cyclical consumer products, which tend to be durable, are often postponed if times are tough. For example, the earnings of automobile manufacturers move sharply during different stages of the economic cycle. Auto makers lost money during the 1980-81 recession, but when interest rates dropped and the economy improved, pent-up consumer demand led to a strong pickup in sales and profits over the following seven years. Then profitability dipped again in the late 1980s and early 1990s, reflecting a weaker economic environment. Another industry that is especially cyclical is homebuilding and related areas.

Some industries are more sensitive to economic cycles than others. For example, property/casualty insurers tend, over time, to have sizable swings in profitability that are linked to industry pricing. When policy prices to consumers are on the rise, insurers are spurred to write more policies and generate new business. Eventually a wave of price-cutting follows, and earnings suffer. The airline industry has similar boom-and-bust cycles. Another example includes the area of electronics, where frequent introductions of new-generation chips have caused big swings in profitability—and highly cyclical stock prices. Investors willing to buy early, when the outlook is still bleak, can enjoy a nice ride up on a cyclical stock.

Defensive. The opposite of cyclicals are defensive industries—those whose products and services are staples of everyday consumer life. People will buy them even in the middle of an economic recession. The earnings of these industries tend to be smoother and more predictable than those of the cyclicals. As a result, these stocks are often seen as a safe haven in a weak economic environment. Defensive industries include food production, tobacco, pharmaceuticals, and soft drinks.

High-Growth. Some industries grow at a significantly faster pace than the U.S. economy. Examples from the past decade include medical equipment and computers. Such areas tend to have rapid growth but also rapid change; new technological developments can lead to overnight success or overnight product obsolescence. High-growth stocks command relatively high P/Es; they may also be volatile. Companies on the cutting edge often see soaring stock prices, but those left behind may see their stock prices quickly fizzle.

Interest-Sensitive. These are industries whose operating results and/or investment appeal are likely to be significantly affected by changes in interest rates. This includes some of the cyclical industries, such as automobile manufacturing and homebuilding, whose sales of big-ticket items are reliant on consumer financing. The operating results of banks are also sensitive to changes in interest rates. If rates go down, banks' cost of funds will likely decline, boosting earnings. In addition, stocks with relatively high dividend yields, the prime example being utilities, tend to benefit when rates decline. As the stock price rises, the dividend yield to a new buyer declines, keeping the yield in line with that available on fixed-income securities.

If a stock portfolio is sufficiently diversified across various industries with different characteristics, the volatility of specific stocks will have a surprisingly small influence on how well the entire portfolio does. Its performance will primarily reflect how strong the overall stock market is and the weightings in industry groups. Some industries have had relatively strong stock performance over lengthy periods, while others have passed in and out of favor. For results of selected industry groups in recent years, see Table 6.

Individual Stock Selection

Approaches to individual stock selection vary. Some investors prefer to emphasize growth stocks—shares of companies whose earnings are expected to rise significantly faster than the general economy. Because such companies are prized by investors, their shares often carry premium valuations. For example, assume two companies (Company A and Company B), each of which is expected to earn $2.00 a share next year. For Company A, however, $2.00 is 25% more than it earned last year, and similar advances appear sustainable for several more years. For Company B, $2.00 is a 5% increase from last year, and no more than 10% rises are projected for the subsequent two years. In such a scenario, the shares of Company A—the growth stock—may be priced at $40 (or 20 times the estimated earnings for the year ahead), while the stock of Company B may be $26 (a price/earnings multiple of 13).

Owning growth stocks can lead to large gains for investors. If, a year later, Company A's shares are still selling at 20 times the expected earnings for the year ahead, the earnings multiple could be based on per share earnings of $2.50, rather than the old $2.00. This would result in a stock price of $50, or a 25% rise in one year's time. Meanwhile, if Company B's stock is selling at 13 times projected earnings of $2.20, its price would be only $28.60. However, growth stocks' premium valuations make the shares vulnerable to sharp declines, particularly if earnings are disappointing.

In addition to above-average earnings growth, characteristics of growth-stock companies often include involvement in new product or service areas; a sizable amount of research and development spending; and a large reinvestment of earnings

TABLE 6: PERFORMANCE OF SELECTED S&P INDUSTRY STOCK GROUPS*

Industry/Sector	Compound Annual Returns (w/o Divs)				Industry/Sector	Compound Annual Returns (w/o Divs)			
	1 Yr.	5 Yrs.	10 Yrs.	15 Yrs.		1 Yr.	5 Yrs.	10 Yrs.	15 Yrs.
S&P 500 Composite	20.3	12.2	11.5	12.7	Household Furnigs & Appl	-9.9	7.8	2.3	8.7
Aerospace/Defense	31.7	25.7	14.1	15.7	Household Products (Non-Dur)	26.4	18.8	17.5	18.4
Airlines	9.5	2.8	3.6	9.1	Housewares	14.7	5.8	14.5	...
Aluminum	12.4	12.2	11.7	9.4	Insurance (Life & Health)	19.2	13.4	10.0	14.9
Auto Parts & Equipment	9.6	12.3	7.8	10.4	Insurance (Multi-Line)	25.2	20.5	11.4	11.9
Automobiles	9.8	20.3	7.2	12.9	Insurance (Property-Casualty)	19.2	14.2	9.5	11.4
Banks (Major Regionals)	32.4	20.5	11.1	7.2	Insurance Brokers	14.9	5.6	3.9	...
Banks (Money Center)	45.9	29.4	11.3	13.0	Iron & Steel	-12.0	8.3	8.8	2.2
Beverages (Alcoholic)	17.4	7.2	12.1	17.5	Lodging-Hotels	18.5	27.8	8.9	12.5
Beverages (Non-Alc)	29.9	19.8	24.7	24.4	Machinery (Diversified)	22.2	17.8	12.8	7.5
Brdcstg (TV, Rad & Cab)	-18.1	13.5	12.8	18.5	Manufacturing (Diversified)	35.5	21.6	14.3	...
Building Materials	16.7	14.4	7.9	12.1	Metals Mining	-0.6	8.1	12.9	6.6
Chemicals	28.9	17.3	11.6	13.6	Natural Gas	29.4	15.2	7.2	8.1
Chemicals (Diversified)	13.4	15.0	11.8	14.3	Office Products & Supplies	23.0	17.7	10.3	...
Chemicals (Specialty)	1.1	7.4	7.6	...	Oil & Gas (Drilling & Equipt)	39.2	12.1	11.2	2.6
Communications Equip	16.7	15.7	17.9	12.4	Oil (Domestic Integrated)	22.3	6.8	6.0	5.6
Computers (Hardware)	32.9	10.6	1.8	6.5	Oil (Intl Integrated)	19.3	12.9	11.7	12.5
Computers (Sftwre & Svces)	55.3	34.0	17.7	22.1	Paper & Forest Products	7.8	8.8	6.9	10.7
Consumer Finance	59.5	28.6	13.6	17.4	Personal Care	45.3	22.8	22.4	19.2
Containers & Pkg (Paper)	17.8	2.5	6.8	13.2	Publishing	-1.3	11.6	6.2	11.8
Containers (Metal & Glass)	25.1	10.4	13.2	18.9	Publishing - Newspapers	24.9	13.9	5.3	11.1
Distributors (Food & Hlth)	-3.6	9.4	9.5	...	Railroads	16.1	15.0	15.2	13.2
Electric Companies	-6.0	0.6	2.5	6.5	Restaurants	-1.9	17.5	13.6	17.6
Electrical Equipment	32.4	19.9	13.2	13.0	Retail (Building Supplies)	17.5	8.4	9.9	...
Electronics (Defense)	21.2	25.6	18.1	...	Retail (Department Stores)	10.6	7.3	9.8	16.3
Electronics (Instrumentatn)	23.4	28.9	14.8	13.8	Retail (Drug Stores)	25.7	16.1	13.6	16.0
Electronics (Semiconductors)	79.4	50.5	27.6	22.0	Retail (Food Chains)	14.3	14.9	16.7	19.7
Engineering & Construction	-8.6	6.1	11.2	...	Retail (General Merchandise)	12.4	3.2	9.9	15.8
Entertainment	1.0	14.3	15.4	15.0	Retail (Specialty Apparel)	40.3	-0.3	6.8	...
Foods	15.7	8.2	13.7	19.6	Savings & Loans	16.6	13.5	6.2	11.5
Footware	65.0	19.7	24.5	22.6	Svces (Commercl & Consum.)	1.9	3.1	1.1	...
Gold & Precious Metals Mining	-1.5	8.3	7.0	4.0	Telecomm (Long Dist)	1.3	12.0	10.9	...
Hardware & Tools	-7.8	8.6	5.9	8.2	Telephones	-3.2	8.9	7.8	...
Health Care (Diversified)	23.1	10.6	14.6	...	Textiles (Apparel)	35.3	3.6	5.0	13.8
Health Care (Drugs - Maj.Phrm)	22.2	11.5	17.7	18.6	Tobacco	21.4	8.4	19.3	20.5
Health Care (HospMgmt)	17.3	16.3	12.0	9.4	Truckers	-26.2	-6.8	-4.0	4.8
Health Care (Med Prods & Sup)	13.5	8.7	12.5	14.3	Trucks & Parts	26.9	13.5	6.0	7.0
Homebuilding	-10.1	6.2	5.1	7.2	Waste Management	4.4	-2.0	5.9	13.0

* Periods ending December 31, 1996. All performance group numbers have been rounded. Excludes 30 groups for which 10 years of history was not available (e.g. Biotechnology, Computers (Networking), and Investment Banking & Brokerage groups). Also, the composition of some industry groups has changed during the periods noted above.

Source: S&P Industry Reports.

into the growth of the business, rather than payment of dividends to shareholders.

A second approach to stock selection is called value investing, which involves looking for stocks of companies whose assets seem undervalued. For example, the cost of replacing or duplicating a company's assets (assuming that someone would want to) may be far more than the value that is suggested by its stock price. In buying such shares, an investor is hoping that other people will come to the same conclusion and that demand for the stock will cause its price to move higher. This could, for example, come in the form of a takeover bid from another firm. Stocks that fit a strategy of value investing frequently belong to companies that operate in relatively mature industries and possess attractive assets such as major brand-name products, real estate, and a strong balance sheet.

Investors should generally have a mix of growth and value stocks. Over the long term, however, the two categories tend to move in and out of favor. As a result, investors have opportunities for sizable gains if they can correctly anticipate and participate in a changing market psychology that causes a greater emphasis to be placed on either growth or value.

Other approaches to stock selection, which may involve an emphasis on growth or value, include choosing stocks with relatively low P/Es or with high dividend yields.

Many successful investors have made much of their fortunes by being contrarians: Contrarians go against the thinking of the crowd. For example, when everyone sells cyclical stocks and the prices are driven down, contrarians buy them. Or, when a blue-chip stock is temporarily out of favor—perhaps the price has dropped because earnings for the quarter were below Wall Street forecasts—value-oriented contrarians will step in and buy. Likewise, if a stock has a sharp run-up because of heavy buying, the contrarian will lighten his or her position. Just as following the pack has its risks, so does contrarian investing. There can be good reasons for certain stocks to drop sharply in price without much likelihood that they will rise again anytime soon.

Looking at Small and Midsized Companies

Small and midsized companies can provide fine opportunities for investors. Often such firms are growing faster than their larger counterparts but are not yet big enough to attract widespread investor attention. Enormous profits have been made by investors who bought some of today's industry giants when they were in their formative stages.

Particularly with stocks of small companies, however, price volatility, or risk, can be much greater than is typical for shares of large corporations. Also, even if an investor uncovers an attractive small-cap stock, there could be a sizable wait before a significant number of other people also become enthusiastic. Institutions such as pension funds tend to be heavily weighted toward the larger companies, and their charters may preclude them from investing in firms whose stock is valued below a certain amount.

Market Indexes

One way to monitor whether stocks are in or out of favor is to compare their stock performance with those of various market indexes. For example, the S&P 500 tracks a broad group of large-company stocks. Both it and the Dow Jones Industrial Average (DJIA), 30 large-capitalization stocks, are indicators of how the stocks of large companies are faring generally.

The S&P MidCap 400 Index provides a view of investors' sentiment toward midsized corporate America. This index includes the stocks of 400 companies (see Table 7), about 30% of which are represented by over-the-counter stocks. Together, the approximately 900 stocks in the S&P 500 and the S&P MidCap indexes represent about 85% of the stock market value given to all stocks traded in the U.S. However, there are thousands of additional stocks, most of which, based on the value given to their outstanding shares, would be considered small-capitalization issues.

Over long periods of time, small-cap stocks have outperformed those of their larger counterparts. However, the price movements of small-cap stocks tend to be more volatile than those of large-cap stocks, and there can be extended periods when investors sentiment favors one group more than the other.

The Appeal of Index Funds

Investors who do not want to select individual stocks can invest in mutual funds that are designed to replicate the performance of the broad market indexes, such as the S&P 500 or the S&P MidCap 400. These are called index funds.

Many pension funds invest a portion of their assets in index funds. One advantage is that transaction costs tend to be low because the

TABLE 7: CHARACTERISTICS OF S&P 500, S&P MIDCAP 400 AND S&P SMALLCAP 600 INDEXES (As of 12/96)

	S&P 500	S&P MidCap 400	S&P SmallCap 600
Total market value	$5.6 trillion	$681 billion	$290 billion
Average market capitalization	$11.3 billion	$1.7 billion	$483 million
Median market capitalization	$5.4 billion	$1.4 billion	$385 million
P/E ratio	20.6	22.9	30.8
Dividend yield	2.01%	1.46%	0.89%

Source: S&P Index Services.

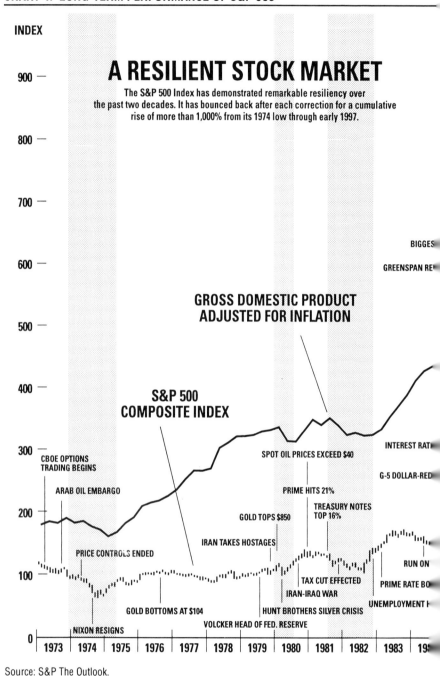

A RESILIENT STOCK MARKET

The S&P 500 Index has demonstrated remarkable resiliency over the past two decades. It has bounced back after each correction for a cumulative rise of more than 1,000% from its 1974 low through early 1997.

GROSS DOMESTIC PRODUCT
ADJUSTED FOR INFLATION

S&P 500
COMPOSITE INDEX

INDEX

BIGGES
GREENSPAN RE

INTEREST RAT
SPOT OIL PRICES EXCEED $40
G-5 DOLLAR-RED

CBOE OPTIONS
TRADING BEGINS

ARAB OIL EMBARGO
PRIME HITS 21%
TREASURY NOTES
TOP 16%
GOLD TOPS $850

IRAN TAKES HOSTAGES

PRICE CONTROLS ENDED
RUN ON
TAX CUT EFFECTED
PRIME RATE BO
IRAN-IRAQ WAR
UNEMPLOYMENT H
GOLD BOTTOMS AT $104
HUNT BROTHERS SILVER CRISIS
VOLCKER HEAD OF FED. RESERVE
NIXON RESIGNS

1973 | 1974 | 1975 | 1976 | 1977 | 1978 | 1979 | 1980 | 1981 | 1982 | 1983 | 19

Source: S&P The Outlook.

GDP
BIL. $

— 7500

FED BOOSTS FED FUNDS RATE
GOLD DROPS TO 4-YEAR LOW OF $339
BUDGET NEGOTIATIONS BREAK DOWN
FED SHIFTS TO EASY CREDIT
DOLLAR SETS NEW LOW AGAINST YEN AND MARK

EST.

— 7000

30-YEAR T-BOND YIELD PEAKS AT 8 1/8%,
REPUBLICANS WIN CONGRESS FOR FIRST TIME IN 40 YEARS
FIRST OF FED'S SEVEN '94-'95 INTEREST-RATE HIKES

— 6500

CK MARKET DECLINE
R AT THE FED

— 6000

30-YEAR T-BOND YIELD HITS 20-YEAR LOW

— 5500

DOLLAR HITS POST-WORLD WAR II LOW
FRIDAY-THE-13TH MARKET PLUNGE
SPOT OIL TOPS $40

— 5000

DISCOUNT RATE CUT TO 3%
USSR BECOMES COMMONWEALTH OF INDEPENDENT STATES
USSR ATTEMPTED COUP FAILS
PERSIAN GULF WAR ENDS
IRAQ INVADES KUWAIT

SCANDAL

R LOW

— 4500

BERLIN WALL COMES DOWN
RJR LBO (LARGEST EVER) ANNOUNCED

IRAN ARMS AFFAIR

— 4000

OIL PRICES FALL BELOW $7 A BARREL

TS HIGH AGAINST D MARK & POUND

LINOIS

— 3500

GH

Shaded areas represent periods of business recession.

— 3000

1986 | 1987 | 1988 | 1989 | 1990 | 1991 | 1992 | 1993 | 1994 | 1995 | 1996 | 1997

stocks that make up an index do not change often, and investments that replicate a broad-based index offer extensive diversity. Also, over the long term, due in part to lower costs, broad-based index funds have provided better returns to investors than most categories of mutual funds.

At the most passive level, an investor can simply own shares of an index fund for a lengthy period of time, seeking to participate in a continuation of the above-average returns that stocks have historically provided.

At a more aggressive level, an investor can try to time the market—to increase the level of stock holdings when the general tide is expected to rise and to sell stocks when a falling market tide seems likely. Successful anticipation of the market's direction benefits owners of index funds, just as it does investors who are choosing stocks on an individual basis. Most stocks are significantly influenced by the direction of the overall market.

Most people, however, have neither the inclination nor the ability to correctly anticipate, on a sustained basis, the many short-term changes in the direction of the market. A middle-level approach involves seeking to identify long-term trends and, perhaps, extreme levels of sentiment, which signal a changing of the tide. For example, extreme pessimism, reflected in such factors as historically low stock prices relative to corporate earnings and dividends, can indicate that a market upturn is ahead. Similarly, relatively high levels of optimism can set the stage for a fall. Investment decisions based on such factors can be implemented through purchases or sales of index funds, other types of mutual funds, or individual stocks.

For most individuals, this emphasis on long-term trends is best (see Chart 4). In a general sense, it involves seeking to benefit from secular and cyclical changes in the economy and the stock market. In a specific sense, it involves selecting an attractive mutual fund and/or a group of individual stocks with favorable characteristics. This long-term approach still requires monitoring choices and judging whether the conditions that made an investment attractive initially continue to exist. If factors change enough, selling the investment may be advisable. With this approach, however, the investor is less concerned with the day-to-day or even month-to-month fluctuations of stock prices. Some stocks may be owned for years at a time, possibly even through some cyclical downturns if appreciation is expected in the future. Underlying factors to consider when deciding whether to retain an investment in the midst of falling stock prices include your level of confidence in the company's management, its financial strength, and its product brands or technology.

Dollar Cost Averaging

As a long-term approach, one of the simplest and most practical stock investment systems is dollar cost averaging (see Table 8). This systematic savings plan is ideally suited to individuals with steady incomes who are able to invest a fixed amount regularly over a period of years. Dollar cost averaging avoids the wide margin for error involved in trying to gear purchases and sales to the swings of the general market. Those who participate in investment programs (e.g., certain ESOPs, 401(k) plans) with set contributions taken from their paycheck each month to buy stock, are using this technique.

Dollar cost averaging merely involves buying equal dollar amounts of stock at regular and continuing intervals, whether annually, semiannually, quarterly, or monthly. An example of dollar cost averaging used on an annual basis is illustrated in Table 8. The simple arithmetic principle involved is that the same amount of money will buy more shares when the price is low than when the price is high. Dollar cost averaging is particularly well suited to blue-chip growth stocks, whose prices tend to move upward in the long term.

Conversely, investors may want to consider systematically cashing in some of their investments. This may be particularly appropriate for older, retired individuals who are increasingly looking to their investment portfolio to meet their spending needs. Rather than relying only on dividends and interest, such investors could supplement their cash flow with regular withdrawals of principal (including capital gains, if any). Many mutual funds will assist in creating a systematic withdrawal plan.

TABLE 8: AN EXAMPLE OF DOLLAR COST AVERAGING

Assuming that an investor has $50,000 to invest, the choices include: (A) buying a fixed number of shares each year until fully invested; (B) dollar cost averaging; i.e., buying a constant dollar amount each year until fully invested.

| Year | Price per share | Choice A | | Choice B | |
		Shares purchased	Dollars spent	Dollars spent	Shares purchased
1	$50.00	200	$10,000	$10,000	200
2	25.00	200	5,000	10,000	400
3	37.50	200	7,500	10,000	267
4	62.50	200	12,500	10,000	160
5	75.00	200	15,000	10,000	133
Totals		1,000	50,000	50,000	1,160
Average cost per share		$50		$43.10	

Source: S&P.

Dividend Reinvestment Plans

Dividend reinvestment plans (DRPs), under which cash dividends are used to purchase additional shares of stock (typically with little or no brokerage commission charged to the individual), are one way to implement dollar cost averaging. More than 900 public companies offer such plans. Companies generally do not charge shareholders a fee for joining a DRP, and some firms offer DRP participants the opportunity to reinvest the dividends at a discount from the prevailing market price (ranging from 1% to 10%). Moreover, many DRPs allow for additional cash purchases at favorable costs (e.g., no brokerage commission) to the investor. In most cases, at least one share must be purchased from a broker in order to participate in a DRP. However, a growing number of companies permit you to buy the initial share from them. Standard & Poor's publishes Directory of Dividend Reinvestment Plans.

Preferred Stock

Preferred stock, which not all companies have, generally entitles the shareowner to receive a fixed dividend before any payment can be made to the holders of common stock. Owners of preferred stock also carry a superior claim against assets if the corporation is liquidated. Some preferred issues are convertible into common stock at fixed exchange rates. Two factors largely determine the value of a preferred stock: the price at which it is convertible into common stock and the level of its fixed dividend. Because the amount of a preferred stock's dividend typically does not change, these shares generally have many of the characteristics of fixed-income securities. Typically, there are smaller price swings with preferred stock than with common stock, so there is less risk. Common stock, however, provides a better way to maximize participation in the potential growth of a company.

Preferred stock is largely owned by institutions and corporations because provisions in the tax laws allow dividends that they receive from preferred stock to be largely tax-exempt. In contrast, dividends on preferred stock received by individual investors are fully taxable. Since most of the demand for preferred shares comes from tax-advantaged buyers, who receive a higher after-tax yield, such stock is typically less attractive than other forms of investments for individuals.

Some Do's and Dont's

Although we recognize that personal circumstances vary widely, below are some general guidelines for stock investors. Much of this advice applies to other kinds of investments as well.

Do's

- Know your objectives and risk tolerance, and look at whether they are compatible with one another. If they are compatible, use them in a disciplined investment approach.
- Diversify among various classes of assets and within individual classes when choosing your investments.
- Distinguish between a company and its stock. There are well-managed companies whose stock price already amply reflects performance and prospects.
- Remember the importance of compounding (see Page 6), and the erosion of purchasing power that inflation can have on future returns.
- Be aware of the extent that fees and taxes can affect the return from your investments.
- Monitor and evaluate the performance of your investments. If your objectives, risk tolerance, or external conditions change significantly, reevaluate your investments. If you buy individual stocks, the establishment of price objectives (subject to change) can be useful.
- Try to be anticipative rather than reactive in your investment decisions.
- Keep good records of your investments.
- Learn from your mistakes.
- Read and stay current with the economic environment and with other factors affecting your investments.
- Be skeptical of rumors and fads.

Don't's

- Don't make any investments that you do not adequately understand or that make you uncomfortable.
- Don't expect too much too soon. Be patient. Even if you have uncovered an undervalued stock, the price is not likely to rise until more people agree with you.
- Don't be married to a stock because you are reluctant to take losses or because you're unwilling to see that a situation has changed. You can improve the overall performance of your portfolio by accepting mistakes and redeploying the remaining funds.
- Don't be too greedy for capital gains. Just because a stock has gone up does not mean that it will do so indefinitely. You might want to set target prices for your investments. Even if you don't sell when the targets are reached, you can reevaluate the stock's attractiveness and decide if a higher target should be set.
- Don't overreach for income. Relatively high dividend yields or interest may indicate a considerable risk that the dividend or interest payment will be reduced or omitted in the future.
- Don't trade in and out of individual stocks too often. Brokerage fees, taxes and other expenses can reduce or even eliminate profits.
- Don't let worries about short-term market fluctuations erode your long-term plan and confidence.

FIXED-INCOME
INVESTMENTS

Characteristics

A bond represents a debt, or an IOU, from the issuing entity to the bondholder. Both governments and corporations borrow billions of dollars from individual investors. The amount of the loan is known as the principal, and the compensation given to lenders for making such funds available is typically in the form of interest payments. As with stocks, there are essentially two ways to make money from bonds: (1) capital gains, which are achieved by selling a bond for more than it cost to buy, and (2) the receipt of periodic interest payments.

Corporate bonds historically have been viewed as safer than stocks. At least in part, this is because bonds have a claim on earnings and assets that ranks ahead of all equity securities in a corporation's capital structure. A bondholder is a creditor of the issuing corporation. A shareholder, on the other hand, is a part owner and is entitled only to a proportionate share of residual assets and earnings, if any. Thus, if financial problems result in the liquidation of a company, bondholders have greater protection in getting at least some return on their investment.

That doesn't mean all corporate bonds are safe. The risk level of bonds in general has heightened during the past several decades, because of wide swings in the interest rates and the sizable amount of so-called junk bonds issued during the 1980s. Corporate junk bonds are issued with significantly above average interest rates, which are typically required to compensate investors for a greater amount of uncertainty about the issuing corporation's ability to meet its scheduled interest and principal payments. Junk bonds were popularized in the 1980s, when many were issued to finance big corporate takeovers. Some junk bonds have provided regular streams of interest payments and have risen in price, but there have also been some sizable defaults on junk bond obligations. Junk bonds are considered noninvestment grade securities, a speculative category that precludes many money managers from owning them.

U.S. government securities include Treasury bills, notes, and bonds. Treasury bills are short-term obligations (mostly with 13-, 26-, and 52-week maturities) sold by the federal government through competitive bidding. Bills are generally issued in $10,000 minimum denominations, then in $5,000 increments above $10,000. These bills are sold for less than their face value, the discount representing the interest. In this respect, these bills are similar to the Series EE Savings Bonds, which are also sold at a discount but are paid off at full face value at maturity. Treasury notes may run up to 7 years, while Treasury bonds typically have maturities ranging from 5 years to 30 years. Interest income on debt obligations of the federal government is typically exempt from state and local income taxes, but is subject to federal taxes. The relatively low credit risk of government securities, plus their favorable tax treatment, causes them to generally provide a lower pretax yield than that of corporate fixed-income securities with similar maturities.

Newly-issued bills, notes and bonds can be bought directly from the Federal Reserve, an approach which provides savings in transaction costs. Also, investors can make individual purchases through a bank or brokerage firm. However, most individual investors typically own such securities through their participation in a mutual fund.

Municipal bonds are issued by towns, cities, and regional and local agencies. They are favored by investors in high tax brackets because interest income is generally exempt from both federal income taxes and those, if any, of the state and locality where the bond was issued. Capital gains on all such bonds are treated as normal taxable income, however. The minimum principal amount of a municipal bond is typically $5,000, although they are sometimes issued at a discount. Growing financial problems facing some municipalities have caused the risk level of certain municipal bonds to increase.

The tax-exempt feature of municipal bonds allows municipalities to borrow money at lower interest rates. These bonds can provide investors with opportunities, on an after-tax basis, to achieve a greater return, for a given amount of risk, than would otherwise be available. To compare the after-tax yields of a taxable bond and a tax-free bond, divide the tax-free rate by the reciprocal of your tax bracket. For example, for an investor in a hypothetical 31% tax bracket, a 6% tax-free bond is the same as an 8.70% taxable yield: computed as 0.06/(1 - 0.31) (see Table 5). Such comparisons should be made among bonds of similar credit quality and maturity dates.

Credit Ratings

A major concern to prospective bond owners is the ability of a borrower to meet its debt obligations. Typically, the interest level of the debt has a close relationship to the borrower's perceived creditworthiness.

The interest rate on U.S. government securities is sometimes called the risk-free rate of return, because the chance that the federal treasury will default on its obligations is slight. Since corporations are viewed as riskier borrowers, they must typically pay a higher interest rate than the U.S. government when they borrow. Lenders want a greater return to compensate them for holding riskier bonds.

Standard & Poor's assigns credit ratings to corporate and municipal bonds. AAA (Triple A) is the highest rating assigned by Standard & Poor's to a debt obligation. It indicates an extremely strong capacity to pay principal and interest. Bonds rated AA are just a notch below, then single A, then BBB, and so on. Some ratings show a + or - sign to further differentiate creditworthiness. A bond with a BBB rating means that the issuer has an adequate capacity to pay principal and interest, but less so than an issuer with an A rating under adverse economic conditions or changing circumstances.

Bonds rated BBB- and above are referred to as investment grade, a category to which certain investors, including many pension funds, confine their bond holdings. Bonds rated BB, B, CCC, CC, and C are regarded, on balance, as predominantly speculative. A bond rating of D indicates payment default, or the filing of a bankruptcy petition. (Other firms also assign credit ratings to bonds, and their opinions and terminology may differ from those of Standard & Poor's.)

Other Factors Affecting Price

More than just the creditworthiness of the issuing corporation influences a bond's price. Returns available from alternative investments, the rate of inflation, and the time line for interest payments and return of principal are also significant factors.

As a general rule, the longer the time to maturity (the date on which the borrower must pay back the principal), the more volatile a bond's price is likely to be. In addition, investors typically require a higher interest rate for long-term debt—whose principal is not expected to be repaid for many years—than they do for short-term debt. This is to compensate them for the greater amount of time that their funds are tied up and for the uncertainty involved.

In large part, interest rates reflect an assumed level of inflation plus a premium for various kinds of risk that lenders take. Unlike cash dividends from stocks, interest payments from bonds (usually distributed semiannually) typically remain fixed over the entire life of the bond. A $100 interest payment received three years from now, however, is not likely to have as much purchasing power as a $100 payment received tomorrow. Therefore, investors generally require a higher yield from longer-term securities. Typically, bond prices rise during periods in which expectations of inflation lower. Conversely, when investors expect inflation to rise, bonds become less attractive to investors and prices generally decline. As Chart 5 indicates, the returns from fixed-income investments tend to weaken during periods of high inflation (e.g., 1979 and 1980, when inflation was at a double-digit annual rate). The returns from U.S. Treasury bills are less volatile, in both directions. This is because, with investors due to receive their return of principal sooner than they will from long-term bonds, erosion of purchasing power, or inflation, is less of an issue.

An attractive feature of bonds (particularly those of higher-quality issues) is the relatively predictable flow of interest and principal payments. The sensitivity of bond prices to changes in the general interest rate environment presents an element of risk to bond traders, however. For example, if an investor elects to sell a bond prior to maturity and interest rates have risen since the bond was purchased, its market price probably will have declined. Alternately, an investor will likely be able to sell at a profit if interest rates have declined.

Reinvestment Rate Risk

If a bond is held to maturity, interim changes in interest rates and bond prices are likely to be less of a concern than if a bond is sold prematurely. However, reinvestment rate risk is a consideration, and that is influenced by changes in interest rates and bond prices. An investor may not be able to reinvest cash returns from an investment at the same level of return with the same amount of risk. This uncertainty about what kinds of returns will be available in the future is the reinvestment rate risk. Thus, even investors who hold bonds to maturity must ultimately face up to changes in the interest rate environment.

For example, during a period when an investor is receiving a 9% annual yield ($90 a year from a $1,000 bond), the interest rate environment may change to the extent that a new buyer of the same bond will receive only a 7.5% yield. Thus, the first investor will not be able to put the $90 to work at the same 9% level unless he or she is willing to assume more risk. Conversely, if rates have risen, it will be possible to invest the $90 at a higher rate of return.

One way many large investors cope with reinvestment rate risk is to establish a rolling bond portfolio. Such a portfolio includes bonds with varying maturity dates, so the whole portfolio won't roll over at once. For example, an investor with $100,000 to be invested in tax-free bonds might purchase ten $10,000 bonds with maturities spaced every 2 years,

CHART 5: ANNUAL INFLATION-ADJUSTED TOTAL RETURNS OF U.S. GOVERNMENT SECURITIES

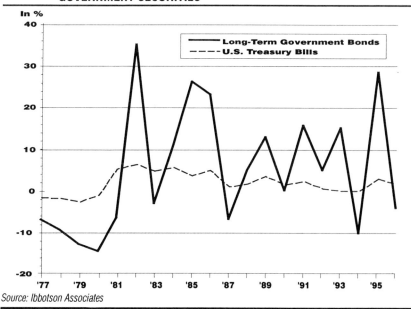

Source: Ibbotson Associates

43

ranging from 2 years to 20. Not only does this diminish reinvestment rate risk, but it also achieves a blended yield of both shorter-term and longer-term returns. In addition, the staggered maturities provide automatic liquidity (from repayment of principal) without having to sell into the market; that is, some money is available every two years.

Some Types of Bonds

Callable bonds.

Many bonds have call features, which give the issuer the right to retire the bond prior to maturity. In such cases, the issuer is enabled, during specific time periods, to call, or repurchase, a bond away from its owner at a preset price that represents a small premium. The action is entirely at the election of the issuer, with no recourse to the holder. Most federal government bonds are not callable; corporate and municipal bonds usually are.

Issuers like the call feature because it gives them opportunities to refinance portions of their debt if interest rates decline. For example, a 20-year corporate bond might be issued at a rate of 11% with a provision that it can be called away from holders after five years at a price of $104 per $100 of principal value. If, five years later, the interest rate for similar bonds has dropped to 8.5%, the issuer would probably find it favorable to call the old bond and replace that debt with a new, and much cheaper, 8.5% bond.

Because of call features, bond investors can be hurt by both rises and declines in interest rates. Regardless of call features, when rates increase, the value of a bond will typically fall, as a means of adjusting its effective yield to that of alternative investments. In addition, a callable bond presents a further problem if interest rates decline enough—perhaps two or three percentage points. In such cases, a callable bond will probably be repurchased from its owner. If that occurs, the investor will be unlikely to find another security of similar quality that will provide as high an income stream.

In addition to looking at characteristics such as creditworthiness and liquidity, therefore, prospective investors should always check on whether a bond is callable and under what terms. Because of this feature, the cash flow stream on callable bonds is somewhat unpredictable.

Convertibles.

One way of counteracting the risk of inflation is to buy bonds or debentures that are convertible into stocks. These securities typically provide many of the safeguards inherent in nonconvertible debt securities yet permit the holder to exchange his or her bond for a specified number of common shares. The advantage of this type of bond is that if the stock price rises, the bond is likely to rise in value also. This kind of upside potential is part of convertible bonds' appeal. Because of this feature, however, a premium must be paid for such bonds: They offer a lower interest rate than regular issues of comparable quality and maturity.

Zero-Coupon Bonds.

Zero-coupon bonds pay no interest until maturity; rather, they are sold at a deep discount from face value and gradually achieve their face value over time. For example, a bond with a $1,000 face value intended to yield 8% over 15 years would be sold initially for about $315. With a zero-coupon bond, you can lock in a relatively assured yield to maturity without having to worry about reinvesting cash interest payments at varying rates in the future. Nonetheless, although the bond owner does not actually receive the cash until the obligation matures, income tax is owed on the implicit interest that accrues each year. Thus, for individual investors, zeros are primarily suitable for IRAs, Keogh plans, and other kinds of tax-sheltered accounts. The most popular zeros are those backed by Treasury obligations.

Inflation-Protected Securities.

The U.S. government is now offering a 10-year note called an inflation-protected security (IPS). The redemption value of the note is subject to adjustment every six months, based on changes in the consumer price index. As a result, when a note is redeemed at maturity, an investor gets back an amount which reflects an adjustment for lost purchasing power (i.e. inflation) during the note's life. However, because of the inflation protection feature, the annual interest to be paid on such notes (prior to redemption) is likely to be less than the fixed level of interest set for ordinary 10-year Treasury notes issued at the same time. The interest on the inflation-protected notes is exempt from state and local income taxes, but, for taxable accounts, federal income tax must be paid on both cash interest payments received plus "imputed" interest (representing inflation adjustments), which will not actually be received until the note is redeemed.

MUTUAL FUNDS

Characteristics

Investors who lack the capital, inclination, or time to establish and maintain adequately diversified stock or bond portfolios often buy shares in investment pools known as mutual funds. Potential advantages of mutual funds include diversification, professional management, relatively high liquidity, and accessibility for people with small amounts of capital. As with individual stocks and bonds, however, there can be wide differences in various funds' performances. Therefore, it is advisable to diversify investments among a few funds with varying objectives rather than buy just one (see Table 9).

As with individual securities, investors should choose among mutual funds based on their personal objectives and risk tolerance. Information about a fund's goals, strategy, performance, management, and fee structure can be found in its prospectus, which investors should read before investing. When evaluating a fund, investors should look at relative performance over various periods of time (for example, 1, 5, and 10 years) and in different kinds of economic and stock market environments. Other factors to look at include the fund manager's experi-

TABLE 9: LONG-TERM CHARACTERISTICS OF MUTUAL FUNDS

	Capital gains potential	Income potential	Total return potential	Risk level
Stock funds				
Aggressive growth	Very high	Low	Very high	Very high
Growth	High	Low	High	High
Income	Low	High	Moderate	Moderate
Growth/income	Moderate	Moderate	Moderate	Moderate
Industry specific	Varies	Varies	Varies	Varies
Precious metals	High	Low	Varies	High
Global	High	Moderate	High	High
International	Very high	Low	High	High
Fixed-income funds				
High-grade corporate	Low	High	Moderate	Low
High-yield corporate	Very high	High	High	Very high
U.S. government	Low	Moderate	Moderate	Low
†Municipal bonds	Low	Moderate	Low	Low
Money market	Very low	Low	Low	Very low

†The income potential and attractiveness of municipal bonds will partly depend on an investor's tax situation.

Source: S&P.

ence and record, the fund's level of consistency, and its major investment holdings. Information and rankings of mutual funds can be found in various publications including *Morningstar, Value Line, Barron's, Business Week, Forbes,* and S&P's *Mutual Fund Profiles* and *Stock Guide.* Some funds do better in certain kinds of environments than others.

Open-End versus Closed-End Funds

Mutual funds fall into two main categories. Open-end funds continuously accept new funds for investment through the sale of additional shares. Also, such funds typically redeem, or repurchase, shares for the current net asset value (NAV) of the shares. The NAV reflects the current underlying value of the securities that the fund owns divided by the number of fund shares outstanding.

Closed-end funds, the second type of mutual fund, raise capital through the sale of a fixed number of shares. Once the initial offering has been made, investors wishing to buy or sell shares of closed-end funds typically do so on the open market, similar to the way most transactions for stocks of individual companies occur. A variety of closed-end funds are traded on the NYSE.

Although shares of closed-end funds occasionally trade above the NAV of the underlying securities that a fund owns, they are more likely to trade at a discount relative to the NAV. In part, this is because many funds have unrealized capital gains on various securities, and the discount reflects the potential tax liability they face when such holdings are sold. Also, with junk bond funds, concern about a fund's liquidity (ability to readily sell the underlying securities at the current market price) can contribute to a discount relative to the NAV.

Many large mutual fund organizations manage families of funds. In such cases, investors can easily switch from one fund to another within the family, with little or no additional charge. This can often be done very conveniently by phone.

Fees

Another distinction among funds is that some charge a sales commission, or load, while others do not. Some funds carry an up-front sales commission, while others charge a redemption fee, or back-end load. This commission, which can cost up to 8% of the initial investment, basically compensates the broker who brings an investor into a load fund. No-load funds do not have commissions, and their shares must generally be bought directly from the fund organization.

Returns to investors are affected not only by fund managers' success in choosing good investments but also by the various kinds of fees that can be connected to fund ownership. Investors should ask themselves, for example, whether a sales commission on a load fund is likely to be offset over time by the load fund's outperformance of various no-load alternatives. For example, a $5,000 invest-ment that charges an 8% load would leave only $4,600 actually being put to work, compared with the full $5,000 in a no-load fund. Over a five-year period, the load fund investment would have to advance about 11.9% annually in pretax dollars to match a return of 10% on a no-load fund. The longer the investor's time horizon, the less significant a sales commis-sion will be to the overall return.

In addition to the commission that may be incurred at the time of pur-chase, other fees may be connected to a mutual fund investment. For example, almost all mutual funds charge an annual fee for managing the assets. Also, some funds have what are called 12b-1 plans that allow them to reduce a fund's assets by 0.25% to 1.25% annually to cover marketing and distribution costs.

Listings of mutual funds can be obtained from the trade associations listed below. These organizations charge a nominal fee for mailing and handling costs.

- *The Investment Company Institute* 1600 M Street N.W., Washington, D.C. 20036
- *Mutual Funds Education Alliance Association of No Load Mutual Funds* P.O. Box 11162, Chicago, IL 60611

International Choices

In recent years, investors have increasingly put money into interna-tional assets. By doing so, they add to the diversification of their portfo-lios and create opportunities to par-ticipate in the growth potential of for-eign economies.

With some nations' economies growing faster than others and with varying political situations, there have been wide differences in returns from various financial markets. Although the economies of various nations are increasingly being linked, significant differences among them still remain. As Table 10 indicates, differences in the performance of various stock markets can be significant from one country to the next and from year to year. In recent years, the overall return from international stocks has substantially trailed that of the U.S.-based S&P 500. In part, this is due to the Japanese market, where the 10-year annual total return from stocks, through 1996, was just 3.3% (mea-sured in dollars), compared to 15.1% from the U.S., according to returns calculated by Goldman, Sachs, & Co. During that same 10-year period, a number of international markets, such as Mexico and Malaysia, provided dollar-denominat-ed returns that surpassed those of the S&P 500. However, U.S. investors should be aware that investing in international stocks may often carry more price volatility (risk) than U.S. equities.

Investors interested in foreign-based stocks have a number of choic-es. One attractive route, which pro-vides both ready-made diversification and professional management, is investing in a mutual fund. Such funds may have holdings from a vari-ety of geographic areas or may con-fine themselves to stocks from a sin-gle country. International funds limit their holdings to markets outside the

U.S., sometimes to a specific region such as the Pacific Rim or Europe. In comparison, global funds typically invest anywhere, including the U.S. Because global funds tend to have 15% to 40% of their assets in the U.S., they are less sensitive to swings in the foreign exchange rate.

In addition, many closed-end mutual funds now focus on a specific country or region. While considerably riskier than the more diversified international and global funds, these country- or region-specific funds also offer opportunities for higher returns if the economy, currency, or other factors cause investor sentiment to swing favorably toward a particular

TABLE 10: ANNUALIZED RETURNS OF VARIOUS NATIONAL STOCK MARKETS (As of December 31, 1996)

Country	1 Year		5 Years		10 Years	
	In local currency	In U.S.$	In local currency	In U.S.$	In local currency	In U.S.$
Australia	14.04	21.76	11.36	12.35	11.13	13.12
Austria	19.29	10.83	4.62	4.29	6.15	8.54
Belgium	22.15	13.17	14.80	14.42	10.83	13.57
Brazil	49.71	4.04	NA	NA	NA	NA
Canada	31.48	30.83	13.58	9.79	9.72	9.80
Denmark	32.04	24.05	7.24	7.27	12.87	15.39
Finland	42.79	34.53	30.60	27.80	NA	NA
France	30.77	23.02	10.86	10.79	9.17	11.42
Germany	27.25	18.19	12.73	12.37	6.57	8.96
Hong Kong	35.29	35.24	27.72	27.87	22.29	22.38
Ireland	26.11	33.17	19.34	18.58	14.62	16.74
Italy	10.97	15.79	10.48	4.45	1.98	0.69
Japan	-5.55	-16.06	-1.63	-0.17	0.18	3.33
Malaysia	25.55	26.22	23.50	25.35	22.15	22.49
Mexico	21.94	19.36	19.33	-1.34	60.97	29.79
Netherlands	37.24	27.19	21.71	21.42	14.88	17.63
New Zealand	11.31	20.30	13.42	19.67	1.53	4.47
Norway	31.98	30.59	14.24	12.70	12.02	13.63
Singapore	3.30	4.46	12.46	15.81	12.72	17.78
South Africa	8.74	-15.25	16.64	7.98	16.37	16.12
Spain	47.61	37.68	18.67	11.83	12.59	12.76
Sweden	42.47	38.28	26.03	20.88	18.21	18.08
Switzerland	19.84	2.70	20.90	21.11	9.33	11.35
Thailand	-40.67	-41.71	NA	NA	NA	NA
United Kingdom	16.10	27.96	15.58	13.54	14.26	15.91
United States	22.76	22.76	15.22	15.22	15.11	15.11
REGIONS:						
World	16.58	13.21	10.54	10.76	9.43	11.02
World excl. U.S.	12.10	6.50	7.80	7.94	6.34	8.75
Europe	24.05	22.98	15.44	13.83	11.19	12.97
Pacific Basin	-0.45	-8.93	1.16	2.87	1.96	5.13

Source: FT/S&P Actuaries World Indices Total Return Data
Note: These total returns have been calculated by Goldman, Sachs & Co. The FT/S&P Actuaries World Indices are jointly compiled by FTSE International, Goldman, Sachs & Co., and Standard & Poor's, in conjunction with the Institute of Actuaries and the Faculty of Actuaries. NatWest Securities Limited was a co-founder of the Indices.

geographic area. Many of the country funds trade on the NYSE or American Stock Exchange (ASE), and some put their emphasis on developing nations with relatively small and volatile equity markets. For the most part, investors interested in long-term commitments should avoid country-specific funds whose shares are selling at a sizable premium relative to the NAV.

Investors can also choose from a number of foreign stocks that can be bought directly on the NYSE or the ASE. The shares of companies such as Sony Corp. and Royal Dutch Petroleum are listed and traded on a U.S. exchange as well as in their home markets. In addition, several hundred foreign companies have American Depository Receipts (ADRs), which trade in the U.S. Though traded like shares of stock, ADRs are actually receipts issued by U.S. banks and trust companies for stocks of foreign companies.

Thousands of other foreign stocks are traded only on overseas exchanges.

Generally speaking, foreign stock exchanges are less liquid than those in the U.S. Also, in some countries political risk factors greatly affect valuations, and foreign taxes may be a consideration. Timely information is more difficult to obtain, and accounting and valuation standards sometimes differ from those in the U.S. This can make it more difficult to compare financial statements and decide when an investment is attractive or should be sold. Transaction costs for buying directly on overseas exchanges are likely to be significantly higher for U.S. investors than for securities bought in this country.

Currency exchange rates, too, are likely to be a consideration when owning foreign stocks because most of the companies have the majority of their sales and earnings in a foreign currency. Although data is sometimes translated into dollars, exchange rates fluctuate. Also, currency movements can directly affect the dollar value of an international asset. If the local currency of a foreign stock weakens against the dollar, the value of that stock is likely to decline when measured in dollars. Conversely, the stock's price, measured in dollars, could benefit if the value of the local currency appreciates.

Given some of the problems that direct investment in foreign stocks can generate, individuals with limited time to research are best advised to stick with ADRs and mutual funds.

In addition to stocks, international investments include fixed-income securities. Again, the investor can choose between mutual funds and individual securities. For those interested, we generally advise choosing a well-diversified mutual fund. Again, factors such as transaction costs and the effect of currency fluctuations should be considered.

Despite the prospect of higher risk and, in some cases, greater transaction costs, a well-diversified portfolio should include some international holdings.

BROKERS AND SECURITIES MARKETS

Although investment choices can appear numerous and complex, the process of implementing a decision once it has been made is generally quite simple. The procedure involves placing an order with a reliable broker or dealer. A transaction can essentially be completed within minutes of placing an order. Sales are usually settled (fully transacted, with ownership and funds changing hands) within five business days.

Functions of Exchanges

Stock exchanges provide a meeting place for buyers and sellers. The exchanges themselves do not buy or sell securities, nor do they fix prices. Prices are determined by means of a two-way auction system.

The most well-known U.S. financial marketplace is the NYSE, where the stocks of more than 2,000 companies, plus many bonds and other kinds of securities, are traded. In addition, hundreds of additional stocks and various other forms of investments are traded on the ASE, which is also in New York City. In addition, transactions are made on a number of regional stock exchanges.

Each stock traded on an exchange is typically allocated to one or more specialist, who is generally expected to maintain a continuous and orderly market in that security. This includes matching buy and sell orders from others. In addition, specialists may also buy or sell stocks from their own accounts to correct temporary supply imbalances between buyers and sellers.

The Nasdaq Stock Market

Aside from those listed on the major exchanges, more than 5,000 stocks are listed and trade in The Nasdaq Stock Market, and several thousand more trade in the over-the-counter (OTC) market.

Unlike the stock exchanges, which require traders to be present on the floor to execute a trade, The Nasdaq Stock Market unites its participants electronically through computers, enabling them to compete in a screen-based market.

And unlike the auction markets of the exchanges, The Nasdaq Stock Market uses multiple "market makers" who compete with one another for investor orders by openly posting the prices at which they will buy and sell shares in which they make a market (bid and ask prices). Because they actually buy and sell shares from investors, Nasdaq dealers act as principals rather than agents.

Several large and well-known companies, such as Microsoft Corp., are listed on The Nasdaq Stock Market. However, Nasdaq is also home to many small companies that either choose not to list on an exchange or do not qualify for exchange listing because of their small size.

Aside from the exchange-traded and Nasdaq listed stocks, the shares of thousands of companies, usually very small or inactively traded, can be obtained in the over-the-counter market. Bid and ask quotes on many of these are reported through an electronic quotation system known as the OTC Bulletin Board.

Regulations for the Securities Industry

The securities industry operates under various federal regulations and ethical standards aimed at protecting investors. Safeguards include requirements for full and fair disclosure in new security offerings. Most public corporations also must file annual and quarterly financial statements so shareholders can monitor how well their companies are doing. In addition, the Securities and Exchange Commission (SEC) requires officers, directors, and principal stockholders of most publicly owned companies to report any of their own transactions in the stocks of their own company.

Aside from federal regulations, most states have laws providing for the registration of brokers and dealers and the offering and sale of securities to the public. In addition, the stock exchanges engage in self-policing, not only in setting standards to be met by companies whose securities are listed but also through prescribing rules of conduct, minimum capital requirements, and so forth, for their own members. In the Nasdaq and OTC markets, the National Association of Securities Dealers Inc. has standards and practices for its members.

Role of the Broker

Assuming you now have a working knowledge of the securities business and are ready to invest some of your money, the person to talk to is a broker. To find one, you may get a recommendation from friends or associates or you can often find advertisements in the financial section of your newspaper.

There are two kinds of brokers—full-service and discounters. With full-service brokers, the commission (transaction fee) is typically higher, but you will likely have access to information and investment advice produced by the brokerage firm's analysts. However, more than one opinion on a prospective investment is advisable before purchasing.

Opening a securities account is relatively easy. It largely involves establishing your identity and depositing enough money to cover the initial purchases you want to make. For higher-risk investing, such as buying on margin, some additional forms need to be filled out, just as when you buy a car or household goods on an installment plan. Your broker's role includes seeking to execute your orders at the best possible prices. If you wish, the broker will keep your securities for you and send you checks for dividends and interest when these are received.

People sometimes feel embarrassed about the amount of money they have to invest. They feel that the broker does not want to be bothered with small sums. However, the NYSE and many larger member firms spend significant advertising dollars to reach small, as well as large, investors. Relatively modest sums may be invested on a periodic basis, particularly in mutual funds but also in individual securities. As illustrated earlier, the power of compounding can build such contributions into a sizable portfolio.

Types of Orders

You can give your broker different kinds of instructions. These include the following:

At the opening
An order left with a broker for execution at the best price obtainable at the opening of the market.

At the close
An order to buy or sell a stock during the last 30 seconds of a day's trading.

Day order
An order good only for the day received, after which it is automatically cancelled.

G.T.C. (Good 'til canceled)
This means that if the transaction is not executed on the day given, the order is carried over by the broker to the following day or to subsequent days until the market reaches the price stipulated or the order is canceled. Other time limits may be designated, such as "good this week," "good this month," and so forth.

Limit order
An order to be executed at a specified price or at a price more favorable to the customer, if possible.

Market order
An order to be executed at the best price obtainable immediately after its receipt by a broker. If not stated, an order is always understood to be at the market price.

Stop order
An order that does not go into effect until the actual market price reaches the price specified on the order. Stop orders to sell are generally placed below the current price, and their most common purpose is to protect the investor against a sudden decline in price. Although stop orders are safeguards, they are not necessarily executed at the designated price, due to market conditions. A stop order to buy is generally placed above the current market, typically to limit the potential loss of a short sell.

Stop and limit
Similar to a stop order, except that the price at which it is executed, after going through the stop, is limited. It is a combination of the stop and limit orders. The limit price may be the same as the stop price, or a different price may be set.

GLOSSARY

Balance sheet – A financial statement that lists values of a company's assets on one side and its liabilities on the other. The liability side of the balance sheet includes both debts of the company and owners' capital. The asset and liability columns always add up to the same amount, hence the use of the term balance sheet.

Basis point – One one-hundredth of a percentage point. This term is often used in describing changes in interest rates. For example, if the yield on a bond has changed from 7.50% to 7.87%, it has moved up 37 basis points.

Call option – The right to purchase a specific number of shares at a stated price within a fixed period of time. A call option, which is the opposite of a put option (the right to sell at a set price), is often purchased when an investor speculates that the price of the underlying security will go up. For each call option purchased, there is also a seller. This is often someone who owns the related common stock. By selling a call option, such an investor is doing a "covered write": a hedge against a decline in the stock price.

Cash flow – Accounting definitions vary somewhat, but one calculation is net income plus depreciation and amortization, which are noncash charges against earnings.

Certificate of deposit (CD) – An investment, often made with a bank, that generally provides a fixed yield for a given period of time, usually six months to five years. CDs usually carry penalties for early withdrawal of funds. Also, tax treatment of income from a CD can be a significant consideration.

Commercial paper – Short-term corporate borrowing that is backed by the general creditworthiness of the issuer rather than by specific assets. Commercial paper is typically sold to financial institutions and mutual funds.

Coupon bonds – These are payable to the bearer, with title passing by delivery without endorsement. Interest is received by clipping the attached coupons as they mature and presenting them for payment. Tax law changes enacted in 1982 effectively prohibit the issuance of such bonds, but preexisting coupon bonds may be purchased in secondary markets.

Coupon rate – The relationship between the annual interest level of a security and its principal amount. For example, a bond with a $1,000 principal amount that pays $80 in annual interest has an 8% coupon rate.

Current yield – The return from interest payments relative to the current price of the fixed-income security. For example, a bond that originally sold for $1,000 may now be selling for $950. If the fixed interest level is $80 per year, the current yield is 8.4% ($80/$950), rather than the original 8.0% yield.

Debentures – Bonds are long-term debt obligations that are secured by specified assets and a promise to pay. Debentures are similar to bonds but are not collateralized, or secured, by specific assets. Debentures are backed by the overall creditworthiness of the issuer.

Depreciation – A noncash expense on a company's income statement that is intended to reflect an eroding value for physical assets such as buildings and equipment.

Dilution – A term typically used in discussing the impact that a transaction has on a company's earnings per share. For example, when an acquisition is made, the financing costs associated with the acquisition may exceed the profits gained from it, in which case there is a dilution of earnings.

Earnings per share – The net income of a company divided by the average number of common shares outstanding in a given period.

Futures contract – A contract to purchase or sell a specific quantity of a commodity, currency, financial instrument, and so forth, at a set price on a stipulated future date.

Guaranteed Investment Contract – A contract in which the issuer makes a commitment to provide interest on invested funds for a period of time. Such contracts are generally issued by insurance companies, and have been used extensively in 401(k) retirement plans.

Hedging – A strategy used to reduce or eliminate investment risk.

Income statement – Sometimes called a profit and loss statement, a financial statement that begins with sales or revenues, then lists major categories of expenses, and ends with pretax income, taxes, and net income.

Initial public offering (IPO) – An opportunity to buy shares of a company whose stock was previously privately held.

Insider – A person close to a corporation who may have access to material, non-public information. This may include officers, directors, large shareholders, and other individuals.

Margin – Partial payment for a security, involving full ownership rights and risks, with the balance financed, usually by a broker's loan. Minimum margin requirements are fixed by the

Federal Reserve Board.

Money market fund – A type of mutual fund that invests in short-term debt instruments, including government paper, commercial paper issued by corporations, and bank certificates of deposit. Some such funds invest exclusively in Treasury securities, and others in tax-exempt securities—passing the tax benefits to shareholders. Money market funds manage their finances to maintain a constant per-share price, generally $1 per share, but their yields change daily, reflecting variations in prevailing short-term interest rates.

Mortgage bond – A bond secured by a mortgage on property, which may be sold to satisfy the debt if the borrower defaults on the payment of interest or principal.

NASDAQ – The National Association of Securities Dealers Automated Quotation system, a computerized communications system that provides continuous price quotations for securities listed on The Nasdaq Stock Market.

Notes – Usually unsecured intermediate- or short-term debt obligations. With reference to U.S. Treasury securities, notes are obligations with maturities of not less than one year and not more than seven years from the date of issue.

Payment-in-kind (PIK) – Typically noncash interest payments, whereby additional debt principal is paid as a form of interest, rather than cash.

Payout ratio – Common share dividends as a percentage of corporate earnings. If a company consistently pays out more money in dividends than it earns, there is a heightened likelihood that the dividend will be reduced or eliminated in the future.

Program trading – Institutional buying or selling of all stocks included in an index on which options and/or futures are traded to take advantage of temporary price variations.

Proxy – Authority conferred by a shareholder that gives another party the right to vote the stock owned by the shareholder.

Put option – A right to sell a specific number of shares at a stated price until an expiration date. A put option is often purchased when an investor expects the price of the underlying security to decline during the life of the option contract.

Registered bonds – Bonds with the owner's name written on their face. They cannot be negotiated except by endorsement and transfer on the books of the issuer.

Retained earnings – Profits of the company that are kept, rather than paid out to shareholders as dividends.

Short sale – A risky investment strategy that seeks to benefit from an expected decline in the price of a stock. It involves the sale of a security the seller does not own, so the seller is borrowing the stock from another party. At a later time, stock similar to that borrowed will be purchased (hopefully at a lower price than it was earlier sold for), so that the lending party's holdings can be restored; this is called "covering" the short position.

Sinking fund – A fixed amount or portion of earnings that an issuer sets aside each year sufficient to provide for the eventual payment of part or all of an issue of bonds or preferred stock. Sinking funds are typically operated by periodically calling portions of the security issue (see the discussion of callable bonds) or by repurchases in the open market.

Stock split – An increase in the number of shares of a corporation through the distribution of additional shares to existing stockholders. For example, in a two-for-one split, each common stockholder ends up owning twice as many shares as were held previously. Once the stock split is declared, the price per share is likely to decline by about half to reflect the greater number of shares in existence. A two-for-one split is similar to receiving two 10-dollar bills in exchange for a 20.

Subordinated – Applied to a bond whose claim on assets and earnings has a lower priority than other debt.

Total Return – Change in price, plus any income received from asset.

Warrants – A certificate giving the holder the right to purchase securities at a stipulated price within or without a specified time limit. Sometimes a warrant is offered with other securities as an inducement to buy.

Yield to maturity – The total expected annual return from interest and principal if a bond was bought at the current price and held to maturity. This assumes that the interest could be reinvested continually at the same rate, which may not be a realistic assumption.

STANDARD & POOR'S PRODUCTS

Standard & Poor's provides a variety of publications and services that are designed to help with investment decisions. Many Standard & Poor's publications include stock opinions from Standard & Poor's STARS, Stock Appreciation Ranking System, a ranking system of approximately 1,100 common stocks.

Standard & Poor's products and services include:

Analyst's Handbook – Compilation of long-term statistics and performance of stock prices for approximately 85 industry groups. Offers convenient opportunity to compare performance of an individual company or a stock to a related industry group. Quarterly data available with monthly updates. Also available on diskette.

Bond Guide – Monthly digest of pertinent information on over 7,000 corporate, foreign, and municipal bond issues. Included are Standard & Poor's ratings on bond quality.

Current Market Perspectives – Monthly publication providing price/volume charts on more than 2,370 widely traded stocks. Also includes relative-strength measurements and three years of data on sales, earnings, and dividends.

Daily Action Stock Charts – Weekly publication with market-action charts on more than 700 stocks, including the majority of the stocks that have the most actively traded options. Includes moving averages, relative-strength measurement, and yearly price ranges for the past 12 years.

Directory of Dividend Reinvestment Plans – Directory listing more than 900 companies that offer dividend reinvestment programs. Features of each plan noted. Includes list of nearly 100 companies that offer discounts from the market price of their stocks for those who participate in their dividend reinvestment plan. Published annually.

Earnings Guide – Monthly publication including quarterly and annual earnings estimates, gathered from 200 brokerage firms nationwide, on more than 4,300 publicly owned companies. Includes high, low, and average estimates, plus other statistical data.

Emerging & Special Situations – Monthly publication, with interim supplements, designed to serve aggressive investors who seek maximum capital gains through equity investments in emerging growth companies, new issues, and special situations.

Industry Surveys – Discussion of recent conditions, trends, and outlook for major U.S. industries. Covering over 50 major industries, it includes semi-annual surveys for each industry, Monthly Investment Review, and monthly Trends & Projections. Also available on CD-ROM.

The Outlook – Weekly publication providing commentary on market trends and investment advice on individual stocks and mutual funds. Includes articles on specific industries and various other subjects of interest to investors. Also includes Standard & Poor's exclusive STARS stock picks.

Index Information Bulletins – Monthly publication available for the S&P 500, MidCap 400, and the SmallCap 600 and 100 Indexes. Each 8-page bulletin provides a list of stocks in the respective S&P Index, with shares, price and market value, performance data, and best and worst performing companies each month.

MarketScope – An on-line electronic service providing updated information on more than 8,000 companies. Includes investment advice, reports on current market conditions, economic data, and various other features of interest to investors.

Stock Market Encyclopedia – Quarterly publication including Stock Reports on 750 companies, including those in the S&P 500.

Stock Guide – Monthly digest of 49 important items of data on more than 7,000 common and preferred stocks. Includes summaries of financial positions, earnings estimates, and stock prices. Also has extensive statistical reference list for mutual fund investors and records of fund performance.

Stock Reports – Five-page reports on thousands of companies. Provide vital facts, figures and projections, including the latest prices, per share data, four-year chart of price ranges, income and balance sheet data, industry data, Wall Street consensus opinions on the earnings outlook, and company news. For 1,100 selected stocks, the Reports have been enhanced with Standard & Poor's Analyst Opinion. Some reports also include a Fair Value rating, Technical Evaluation, Insider Activity and more. Also available on CD-ROM.

Trendline Chart Guide – Monthly publication offering charts on 52-week price performance of more than 4,400 stocks. Includes 30-week moving averages, exclusive relative-strength measurements, and additional information such as earnings per share and indicated dividend rate.

For information on these and other Standard & Poor's products, contact:
Standard & Poor's
25 Broadway
New York, NY 10004
1-800-221-5277

ADDITIONAL READING

Books

Bogle on Mutual Funds
By John C. Bogle
Irwin Professional Publishing

BusinessWeek's Annual Guide to Mutual Funds
By Jeffrey M. Laderman
McGraw-Hill

Classics . . . An Investor's Anthology
Edited by Charles D. Ellis
with James R. Vertin
Dow Jones-Irwin

Competitive Advantage: Creating and Sustaining Superior Performance
By Michael E. Porter
Macmillan

The Dividend Rich Investor
By Joseph Tigue and Joseph Lisanti
McGraw-Hill

Dun and Bradstreet's Guide to Your Investments
By Nancy Dunnan
Harper & Row

Global Investing... The Templeton Way
By Normal Berryessa and Eric Kirzner
Dow Jones-Irwin

Graham and Dodd's Security Analysis
By Sidney Cottle, Roger F. Murray, and Frank E. Block
McGraw-Hill

The Handbook of Fixed Income Securities
By Frank J. Fabozzi, T. Dessa Fabozzi, and Irving M. Pollack
Irwin

How to Make Money in Stocks
By William J. O'Neil
McGraw-Hill

The Intelligent Investor
By Benjamin Graham
Harper & Row

Investment Analysis and Portfolio Management
By Jerome B. Cohen, Edward D. Zinbarg, and Arthur Zeikel
Irwin

Investment Analysis and Portfolio Management
By Frank K. Reilly
The Dryden Press

continued

Managing Investment Portfolios:
A Dynamic Process

Edited by John L. Maginn and Donald L. Tuttle
Assn. for Investment Management and Research

The Mathematics of Investing
By Michael C. Thomsett
John Wiley & Sons

The Money Masters
By John Train
Harper & Row

One Up on Wall Street
By Peter Lynch with John Rothchild
Penguin Books

Portfolio Management and Efficient Markets
By Peter Bernstein
Institutional Investor

A Random Walk Down Wall Street
By Burton Malkiel
W.W. Norton & Co.

SBBI Yearbook
Ibbotson Associates Inc.
P.O. Box 97837
Chicago, IL 60678-7837

Stocks for the Long Run
By Jeremy C. Siegel
Irwin Professional Publishing

What Works on Wall Street
By James P. O'Shaughnessy
McGraw-Hill

Magazines

Business Week

The Economist

Financial World

Forbes

Fortune

Newspapers

Barron's

Financial Times

Investor's Business Daily

The Wall Street Journal

Also worth considering is membership in the **American Association of Individual Investors** (P.O. Box 11092, Chicago, IL 60611-9737), which includes a subscription to its *AAII Journal*, published 10 times a year.